For Miz

In Response to
your wonder full
Book of Days
Here's my book
of years

Love,
Phil

periods,

selected writings 1972-1987

Phil Demise,
Phil Smith

gegenschein press
new york

Printed in the United States of America
 Published 1987.
ISBN: 0-943783-00-3

Cover Art by: Laurel Marx

Some of these poems first appeared in the following magazines and presses: MEASURE (one page novel), ASSEMBLING ASSEMBLING, INTERSTATE, BURNING DECK (Letterpress Pamphlet), BEYOND BAROQUE, CLOWN WAR, FLORA DANICA, NRG, AIEEE, GEGENSCHEIN, davinci, STOOGE, DRAMATIKA, DOVETAIL JOINT, B.G. NEWS, WHITE ARMS MAGAZINE, GLASSWORKS, FERVENT VALLEY, NOTBOOK EDITIONS.

I would like to thank my sister Harriet Kanstroom for 'proofing' that this manuscript was far from perfect and less than punctuated.

I want to acknowledge Irwin J. and Mikka for everything.

GEGENSCHEIN (#23)
one one one third avenue #12C
new york, new york
one zero zero zero three

For

my parents and my transparency
my sister and my system
my brother and my other
my wife and my rifle
my son and my sunset
my friends and my frenzy
my pets and my petulance
my 'oh my' and my goodness

A man (1947-1987),

OTHER BOOKS by Phil Demise/Phil Smith

THE PIPER'S DREAM (1971)
MULTIPLE FRACTIONS AND CONFUSIONS (1972)
THEY THE TWO (1974)
BICENTENNIAL PIECE OF MIND w/Guy Beining (1976)
GREAT NOVEL AMERICAN PERHAPS (1977)
WHAT I DON'T KNOW FOR SURE (1978)
WHITE RUSHES (1979)
MANINFESTED (1979)
EINSTEIN'S RELATIVES/FIGURING OUT NEWTON
w/Dave Zimmer and Renna Zimmer (1982)
ICE ELATION (1983)
MUTTER EI w/tape (1985)
HOME/BODIES w/Dave Zimmer and Renna Zimmer (1987)

for Bitty,
partner in time

CONTENSE

pe·ri·od (pēr′ē əd), *n.* **1.** a rather large interval of time that is meaningful in the life of a person, in history, etc., because of its particular characteristics: *a period of illness; a period of expansion for a company; a period of social unrest in Germany.* **2.** any specified division or portion of time: *architecture of the period 1530–1800.* **3.** *Educ.* a specific length of time during school hours that a student spends in a classroom, laboratory, etc., or has free. **4.** a definite, timed part of a game: *a rest between periods.* **5.** *Music.* a division of a composition, usually a passage of eight or sixteen measures, complete or satisfactory in itself, commonly consisting of two or more contrasted or complementary phrases ending with a conclusive cadence. **6.** *Geol.* the basic unit of geological time, during which a standard rock system is formed: comprising several epochs and included with other periods in an era. **7.** *Physics.* the duration of one complete cycle of a wave or oscillation; the reciprocal of the frequency. **8.** *Astron.* **a.** Also called **period of rotation.** the time in which a body rotates once on its axis. **b.** Also called **period of revolution.** the time in which a planet or satellite revolves once about its primary. **9.** a round of time or series of years by which time is measured. **10.** a round of time marked by the recurrence of some phenomenon or occupied by some recurring process of action. **11.** the point of completion of a round of time or of the time during which something lasts or happens. **12.** *Physiol.* a time of the month during which menstruation occurs. **13.** the time during which anything runs its course. **14.** the present time. **15.** the point or character (.) used to mark the end of a declarative sentence, indicate an abbreviation, etc. **16.** a full pause, as is made at the end of a complete sentence. **17.** a sentence, esp. a well-balanced, impressive sentence; a periodic sentence: *stately periods.* **18.** *Class. Pros.* a group of two or more cola. —*adj.* **19.** noting, pertaining to, evocative of, imitating, or representing a historical period or the styles current during a specific period of history: *period piece; period costumes; period play.* [late ME *peryod* < ML, L *period*(*us*) < Gk *periodos* circuit, period of time, period in rhetoric, lit., way around. See PERI-, -ODE[2]]

—**Syn. 1.** interval. See **age. 2.** term.

There is a precise moment in time
When a man reaches the exact center of his life,

Robert Desnos

Guy R. Beining

INTRODUCTIONS

When I war a baby

When I was a little baby
I always made a fuss and then
stand up on my bed and play with
my little bus.
When I learned to talk I also learned
to walk. when my mother went
out I would shout mommy I won't
make a fuss if you buy me one bus.
and that's the story of part of my life.
and I hope I have a nice wife
and nice children like me and then tell
it to their family.

VERY FORWARD

I am definitely not Dada. I am not neo, pre or post anything. This is who I am. I am no more, probably less, than the definition of these pages. My life's reflections mirror a unique alternative, never to be duplicated. Though my chain of events, like a chromatic gene, replicates and spirals momentarily, its makeup changes its mind and alternates like a newborn. Even (or uneven) at the depths of my despair, I am happy to be who I am, winging a lifetime of larks, dying over and over to stay alive. I am the personification of a human being being a person.

I love to keep myself on my toes, dancing a ballet of unknown origins. Full circles are happy circles. My life has always been from 'now on,' wrapped up in a familiar spiral that gently turns itself inside out and brings my past into my present thoughts about my future beginnings and ends. This continuous simultaneity slips down the funnel and drips into my cup, one drop at a time. The universe slips through its net, at one with its parallel children. I remain on the surface of deep contemplation.

The common denominator pursues an uncommon philosophy which comes upon the simple revelation that is absolutely, almost correct. It is the philosopher who cannot define the words who has a definite edge in the Race (I bet on the one who doesn't even know he's in the Race). The winner is the one who starts slow, takes his time and through the spokes of the unspoken cycles, spins a web of history in his own image.

There is a serious flaw in the idea of a ceiling that lies between two floors. Is it the uppermost? Is it the top? Has the true meaning of ceiling and floor crept into the thickness that resides in between? Can the footsteps on my ceiling be the bottom line in a world of opposites? Can two extremes engage in a marriage of extreme singularity? Can the world and all its petty contra-dictions find the one meaningful language in a dictionary without definition? Can that definition be a shadow of yet another dictionary, spiraling up into its own bottom? If the real suspension of disbelief hanging over my head is someone else's proof of gravity, then why can't the inside be the outside and the present be the future and the left be the right and the right be wrong?

There are those who know and those who know better.

It seems as if a lot of people miss my boat, looking at my impressions as something more than momentary indentations that, due to their lightness, float on the deep end, giving buoyancy to the sinking feelings of day to day existence. I have always had a need to make my impressions known (at the very least, to myself) by placing them outside their intuitive nests and into the open air. I have always liked letting my language take me for a ride, skirting issues that thought and second thought could never explain to my satisfaction. The 'body' has always been the vessel that best represented and best suited this macrocosmic voyage into the deep, dark space of my conjunctions.

Looking back at the whole body, the whole universe of my journey, it appears as a vertical listing of separate excursions, of different moments, each entry describing a reflection of time and each reflection redefining my vision in order to adapt to reality's ongoing distortions. I have "dedicated my life to my life," which by its very nature, mirrors the times I have lived through and reflects what is partially shared by all and partially individual to me. Our experiences are of different degrees and in different contexts but our responses to them are always human and similar. This individual universality *is* the human condition.

Life has, on occasion, been on my critical list but I have only considered giving up the habit 2 or 3 times and then, only on the surface of that finality with any deeper consideration being shut down immediately by a stronger, deeper mechanism.

I intend to be here for the duration of my life. No more, no less.

This collection is my attempt to put forty years between two covers, placing it on my shelf along with the rest of Time. It is defined by its own dimensions; a punctuation in the middle of my sentence, a period in the middle of my life,

Phil Demise, Phil Smith
New York City

1,

19th century Romanticism posited the poet as his own hero -- in his heightened self-consciousness and lucidity, observing his own psychic processes, then trying to record them.

20th century found an extension of this Romantic ideal in Surrealism and Dada -- from Apollinaire who coined the word "surrealism", and Andre Breton who wrote the first SURREALIST MANIFESTO (1920) and described surreal art as "pure psychic automatism ... Dictation of thought without any control by reason, and outside any aesthetic or moral preoccupation ..." That was added to later (1929) in Breton's second SURREALIST MANIFESTO when he described:

> ... a vertiginous descent within ourselves, the systematic illumination of hidden places, and the progressive darkening of all other places, the perpetual rambling in the depth of the forbidden zone ...

Needless to say, Surrealism and Dada have never been popular mediums in America, where the masses like things upfront in fast foods, DAILY NEWS, and TV game shows. A few managed to perservere: Gertrude Stein echoed back to us from Europe; Dali racked up in galleries and advertizing; and on home soil, we had Kenneth Patchen, Jackson Mac Low, Richard Kostelanetz, Allen Ginsberg in fits -- all of them trying for immediate notation, simultaneity of psychic processes, a kind of intuitive cubism in words.

Now we have Phil Demise, with this important full-length book, PERIODS,.

Mind you, to be a Surrealist or a Dadaist is not merely to put words down on paper in an extra-ordinary way -- go back and see how Breton insists that it is first and foremost an inner process, before it gets to notation. This means that to be an authentic Surrealist or Dada poet, one has to live one's life in an extra-ordinary way, and one has to see oneself living that life in an extra-ordinary way, also. Without that, any poet's notations on the page will be pretentious impertinence, and it's pretty easy to sniff out the fakers who try to get away with simple word placements in a kind of pseudo "experimental" poetry.

Phil Demise is no faker and he does not write experimental poetry. He is a born poet and he is simply doing what he knows best to do. He has lived, and is living an extra-ordinary life, and he has seen, and is seeing himself living that life in an extra-ordinary way. He studied poetry at Bowling Green and Queens College; he organized poetry readings at CBGB in the East Village; he published his own magazine, GEGENSCHEIN. He has suffered and grown, grown and suffered, and he has recorded that suffering and growth in the most immediate notations imaginable: endless words and word arrangements; lists; phrasings; letters to god; poems and prose and prose poems and poem prose -- and always there has been strong autobiography and immediacy and simultaneity, running always through all his work. He takes you with him on his vertiginous descents within himself.

The reader who is out for the purest of purest poetry will find it here, not only in spectacularly resonant lines like the following:

Bills mount and multiply like bulls and cows ...

* *

Take me to the Paris of your body ...

* *

telephone wires are for the birds ...

... stiff winter commas

* *
vaseline
syzygy

Not only in lines like the above, but also in the visual arrangements of these lines, poems, fragments, phrasings, listings, communiques. As if Prospero had kept a memo pad by his bed.

"PERIODS" -- the word evokes associations in our minds: women have fertility periods; periods are measurements of time; periods are those dots that tell us when a sentence has finally ended.

Phil Demise loves words, he loves etymological word plays, he loves to play "hide and seek with definition", he loves the germinality of it all. But there is a deeper process at work here, that is going on inside: he breaks words down the same way he breaks inner impressions down. The method is surrealism, the metaphor is splitting atoms in order to release energy.

Some people will hate this book; they can go back to their MacDonald hamburgers. These poems have a purity and an innocence and an uncertainty that is beautiful and terrifying, terrifying and beautiful, to behold.

William Packard

2,

In *Periods,,* we can not only trace the poet's progression, within the realm of poetics, but also watch the growth of his ideology, as applied to the Dada strain. There is also a third path to follow, and that is of a person logging in his thoughts from age twenty-five until months within his fortieth year. In his introductory notes Phil Smith mentions that he has dedicated his life to his life, of which his writing is one large-sized floating chunk. He appears to be swimming inside a bowl of Campbell's alphabet soup only to find that the shore is but a rim, and so he must keep flapping in order to stay afloat.

How much of a Dadaist is this Dada-man? In this nearly 360°, 360 page work, we find anti-social and anti-art qualities. Reason, order, and discipline are tossed to the wind, and the old Dada remedy of chance also plays a part. One senses that there is no link between language and reality. Phil Smith hangs his words out to dry on a line and in the arrangement of whiteness (stark), and blueness (overview) he gives the line a jerk. At times he is on a blindman's run, with the mirror onto AND, ie. DNA, thereby giving us one of his shorter pieces. He packages words into a plastic poetry, via Arp. The pun is uppermost, and that is his little yes wrenched from the big NO. He too, is involved in a moral revolution as opposed to being a part of another ism. One could therefore easily fall into the trap of calling his work pure Dadaist in aim. Almost, but no Magritte pipe will you get, for if you read his piece *Dada Manifested* carefully, there is a two-edged sword being sharpened here.

Such poems as *An Old Flame, May I Have This..., Cheek in Tongue, She Shells, Love You to Bits, Mocean* (for the title alone), *Page Two, Just like that # 4, The Color Scheme* (for the artist Herm Freeman), and the last two pages of *Great Novel American Perhaps,* can all hold there own to any map, or furious range of poetic writings.

Read this book for the pure wonder of wondering.

Guy R. Beining
12/1/86

3,

2/20/87

Dear Phil : Like most of your other literary brothers I have been shocked, elated and depressed by your experience manifested in print and song. I cast my mind's eye back to the future and apprehend the famous "Save the Dodo" benefit concert at Herm Freeman's country estate, circa '78. Only an accomplished pataphysician (doctor my eyes!) like you, could suggest the dodo, well known cultural symbol for the demise of an entire species might yet be *alive*! The pejorative connotations of "dodo" as synonymous with bozo, blockhead and blunderbus indicate that, like us, the dodo is yet held accountable for his stupidity which, it is commonly believed, led straight to his death. "Dead as a dodo," as you know, is deader than dead -- deader even than dear old Dada, Moma, Guggenheim and even, perhaps, Gegenschein? As I stood on the lawn at Herm's place that fine, bright day in the long ago, I doubtless pondered the significance of "Smith's" transformation into Demise and resurrection. Does my memory fail me or did we indeed entreat the American Museum of Natural History to pry open a habitat showcase and permit the band to be photographed amongst their ancient feathered friends? Expecting a mini Woodstock but confronting a mini Dachau, I retreated into the kissing booth manned (womaned) by the lynx who goes by the name of Robin Person. This, I presume, explains my first response to your body of work -- that of shock -- and the shock has a lot to do with mortality. But bodily deaths, as we are taught by Phil Demise (Dem Eyes!), "actualize" what you do do (Dodo song). The theme of Dodo and Doody in your life and work is obviously a subject more suitable for a deconstructive literary scholar than this humble graduate of Pataphysical High School where, as you know, I majored in cafeteria and gas engines. My elation, however, has invariably been provoked by your rise and fall which is why I always loved your Zen title for the appropriately moribund Dodo documentary film project,

"Drop from the Top." How joyous I was to celebrate the arrival of the issue of GEGENSCHEIN that wasn't published at St. Clement's Church that other happy night in '79. So while I think I fully understand the depths to which you have sunk as your relentless biological images slide straight into a seeping, festering, frightening place, you are, to me at any rate (as much as you are like Jarry) also a sentimental case like Walt Whitman who sang the body electric long before the coming of the national guitar. Phil, you know you have my recognition and admiration as a writer, father, husband and a persistent genius in all matters having to do with art, sport and sex. May your garden continue to grow.

Your friend,
Henry Korn

4,

I met Phil Smith somewhat less than half of the way through this huge volume. He was hawking *Bicentennial Piece Of Mind* postcards at the Small Press bookfair at Lincoln Center in 1976. I walked over to him because he had very long frizzy black hair and a funky little imperial beard. At that time I had very long frizzy red hair and a funky little imperial beard.

In my excited frenzy I said, "I don't care what you do, I'm interested." I don't remember him laughing, he just knew what I meant. He told me that he had a band, the N. Dodo Band, and I, sight unseen, booked them into a series of poetry readings and concerts that I was co-running in Prospect Park. I didn't show up at their concert but a friend of mine told me that that was the band that I wanted to join. (I didn't even know that I wanted to join a band). I booked the N. Dodo Band again and this time I went to the show. It *was* the band that I wanted to join. I went and bought an alto saxophone and practiced for a month and then went to Phil's loft and told him that I wanted to be a member of the Dodo Band and he said okay and that began our long friendship.

Here it is ten years later and we have collaborated on many projects but this is the one I am most proud of. Phil asked me to write one of the many introductions to a collection of his poetry. This task requires that I critically read his work. No problem, I have been doing this for ten years.

Phil's work is: Funny, the language sings, touching, and all the things that great poetry is supposed to be, and more than that it is Phil's and Phil's alone. Sure there are influences, he'll tell you that, but there is really only Phil.

I have recently completed twenty poems that are totally immersed in the style of Phil Smith. They reside somewhere on the *edge of meaning*. This phrase has been used by Phil to describe his work and I understand it well enough to finally plagiarize it. When I finished revising my poems I didn't know what they meant, I only knew that the internal logic was consistent and that the language made sense to itself.

What those and these poems were about did not matter.

"art is a personality, a noncommunicative
beast, that is, unable to speak but when
observed a presence comes to mind"
NOWISM MAN INFESTO - Sublet 1974 Summer NYC

"meaning is a definitive disease
meaningless is an infinite antibody"
SSTRANGED - East 9th Street/Paris Spring 1975

"When words swallow their own meanings things made
more than sense."
GREAT NOVEL AMERICAN PERHAPS - MacDougal Street
Fall/Winter 1974 NYC

I believe that Phil's work is inherently spiritual. The amount and the extreme nature of the paradoxes surpass the mundanity of synesthesia and out of body experiences.

"our mouth is full of dreams   a network of invisibility
a bag of distance hangs from our forehead and rattles
with a seductive silence..."
LOOP D. LOOP - East 9th Street Spring 1975 NYC/Paris

"What is the thing whose shadow is the universe?"
PRECIPICE AT THE HEIGHT OF GLORY - Placenter
1976-1978 NYC

"and there we sit
on the tip of almost"
1980 - 14th Street B.T. Oct 1978-1980

Nothingness is not nihilism in Phil's hands but instead the ecstatic ground (sight/site) of meditation.

"no thing is not nothing, it is pure light,
..., nothing is space where things and no
things coincide"
NOWISM MAN INFESTO - Sublet 1974 Summer NYC

"The knowledge of nothingness does not dissolve the body
and that is the physical dilemma in a nutshell."
NUTSHELL - East 9th Street/Paris Spring 1975

Phil says that a poem is one page of an autobiography and I tend to agree. When his life is going well the poems reflect that and likewise vice is versified. The flipping off of one life ruffled through Phil's papers and the taking on of a new skin gives him a rash. Here is Phil's written life and a good one it is. I am happy to be a part of it.

Dave Zimmer

5,

How I remember Phil Smith: slim as an avocado, he liked langostinos and boo, could dance the Tia Maria and the Bela Lugosi, and charmed the trees like a man doing algebra in the Sahara. His music had mojo and was made of Cajun shrimp and crawdads with hot sauce, and spun as elegantly as glaciers slowly swirl and squeal down a mountainside, dark, groaning rivers. The lights of the alphabet shone in his eyes and the secrets of the white undersides of words rose like smoke from the page. The sounds are art, and art is made in the face of death, and death smiles like an old man falling to sleep in a dream of his youth, and a warm woman enveloping him. The old lore? The new lore? What matters is that the moon rises now, and no one cares how far away it is. These poems come from the moon's dark side, where the fires are.

Howard McCord
El Paso, Texas
1987

6,

The best way to approach Phil Smith's poetry is to stage the obvious again. It has its traditions in the central questions of language and its utility. We have all known for millenia that words are not things. They describe the world; they are at least one step from Reality. They are simpler, more discrete, more autonomous, more measurable than Nature. They are a lie that writers must both tell and deny to approach the Truth. Mystics like Akiba and Mohammed have told us that Heaven cannot be netted in words; we know this is equally true of Earth. Even practical Sciences are theoretical because the facts can neither be gathered into a web, nor described accurately. Freud tells us that the mind perceives laterally as well as analytically, that the Unconscious contains the metaphorical associative powers which sometimes rule our existence. Jung emphasizes the paradoxical, contradictory character of all Truth; words in being what they are, and not what they are not, are for this savant a treachery. From all sages and even a few fools we are told that language is a cheat and a folly. Even our neural perceptions are implodings of infantile sensory modes that become organized at the expense of some large, more fluid sanity. Clearly, language to be honest must be allusive as well as direct; it must connect by implication what grammar and syntax make linear and discrete. This is the sort of verse you will be reading in this volume.

Phil Smith does things with language that mock the claim of tyros and churls that words are things. He mocks, he is at the verge of sense, he introduces the reader to geographies where things blend into other things, he makes language a ritual comedy. The book is a sort of memoir, and sometimes is quite straightforwardly a prose record of his life. Most of the time the language demands the reader react in an alert and involuted way to get the *effect* of the words. Such approaches tend to lead to exploration of words as a kind of music, and Phil Smith has extended his researches into a form all his own that is not rock, not the usual electronic drone, but a sound with formal and insinuating elements- like his poetry. The aim of his Art is not to be clever, but to be clear. Sometimes clarity occurs just when everything is unthinkable, or merely obscure. This poetry is fun. Always amusing, it is never one to insult the reader by being didactic, or lacking astonishment. It preaches, it surprises, it is always entertaining.

Matthew Paris

7,

THE BOUNDARY HUNTER PHIL DEMISE

Neo neo. For Phil Demise, one word around things is never enough. As a true believer in another kind of religion, he avoids the one reading/meaning/voice/definition of his rituals. The early "dictionary" work is filled with odd fusions; the result of placing one thing next to another. It is here that he stakes out his claim to contradiction (contra/diction). Or, as he put it so well: "Circumstance has a mind of its own." (...and a meaning, too, albeit changeable.)

Phil Demise conducts a one-way conversation with meanings that are barely hanging onto themselves. He challenges us with his mixed metaphors and mixed (up) feelings. But once stated, they are hard to erase. They can't be taken away from our world. They contribute to the contradictory atmosphere of our life. It is not so much a style as a state of mind. He is not Dada, nor neo, etc., but rather like a friend in a faraway place.

Phil sees chaos and collaboration wherever he goes. He might ask: "What if Michaelangelo's *Pieta* were to somehow coincide with Hamlet's discovery of the crime in *Hamlet*?" He confuses us! His ideas go against the grain. And if one answers, "Let's talk about specifics, let's account for the facts, let's try to make sense!" - on that he has absolutely nothing to say!

First he might imagine that everything is fine, and then he gives us the impression of hopeless longing. He disorganizes our emotions. He maintains no preference, taking things just as they are, or aren't, or might be, or not! Through this, he creates word-and-alphabet-scapes of tension and relaxation. His world is flat and sparsely populated, like a Dubuffet painting. And in this world, a rule of thumb prevails: We think too much too little, and/or we think too little too much.

In all, we are reminded of the similarity to ourselves. Do you recognize the concept? An absurd experiment written in a strict format. Like a mirror he tries to say something about...uh...our...uh...THE SITUATION!

The boundary hunter Phil Demise comes to destroy meaning, but allows in its place a new disorder. Courage is his method: the courage to put one thing next to another, the courage to quote chaos, to be pataphysical, to let it happen: asserting itself by itself, by the courage of its having been finally done, of his having done it. Courage is the way. Demise Lives.

Herm Freeman
Westport, July 1987

8,

I DOT NO WT ME PADDYS PORTRO
MES WNET S MA LOT OV THES
BT I LOVE ME DAD POETO
I LK THE PHA HT THEYS MAK.

TRISTAN SMITH
NEW YORK, 1987

(I don't know what my daddy's poetry means when it means a lot of things but I love my daddy's poetry. I like the pictures that the words make.)

IN MY FATHER'S MEMORY*

are the cumulus stoops of Time
is the fearful sleep of continuity
was the future of my memories

are the childish images of recollection
is the practically absent dream
was the familiar backdrop of connection

are the buried surfaces of meaning
is the open ended tunnel
was the backyard of nostalgia

was, is

the singular embrace of a parallel universe

(**fue* : to be or not to go
my sister's vision
the preterit tenseness
the absolute past
the *not* imperfect continuance)

TO MIRIAM

NO ONE CAN BE DESOLATE WHEN
ANOTHER'S HEART
IN PULSING QUICKNESS RESPONDS
UNTO HER OWN
DESPAIR IS BUT THE EAGER
PAINFUL DART
OF UNFED HOPE STRAINING TO BE
FULLY GROWN
IT CAN GIVE FIRE AND COURAGE TO
ALL THE WEAK
FOR RESOLVED TO DIE ONE CAN FEAR
NO MEN
BUT RUSH ON ALL ONES FOES TO
VENGEANCE WREAK
AND THUS THEY DIE AND ALL HER
SPIRIT SHINES AGAIN
SO BEWARE MY DEAR OF ANY
DESPERATE STEPS
THE DARKEST DAY IF BUT WE
LIVE TILL MORROW
WILL HAVE PASSED AWAY AND WITH
IT ALL ITS SORROW.

god

I think god is a nice guy and he's way
way up in the sky. he makes everyone
like you and me everybody lookes at
him but never can see. he made the
fish he made the flowers and lets
the rain fall down in showers

In my prayer I always say that the guy
for me every day

So young were the words that their sense slipped off the skin

Tristan Tzara

Phil Demise

ACADEMISE
1972-1974
BOWLING GREEN, OHIO

Academise 1972-1974

In my second chance at further education, R and I arrived on the flat table of Bowling Green, Ohio in the summer of 1972. The two years here were my most youthful and flamboyant. The fantasy, unchained and cushioned by the community, was lived out to the fullest. It was as if there was no future- just an ongoing present, going on and on. I wrestled, often in a stupor, with the 'image' of art. That life was to be Art and anything that might look good in a biography was to be considered and most times committed. R and I shared this dark, youthful romanticism.

The years, though singed with Quaaludes and post-marital sexual experimentation (1970's style) were also filled with great discoveries of the distant echoes of my own voice. I finally became a 20th century poet. I found myself 'as is' with an unquenchable thirst for discovering new ways of saying the same things. My influences were direct, live and in person. Contact with Howard McCord, Ray DiPalma, Tom Raworth, Anselm Hollo, Richard Kostelanetz, William Packard and David Meltzer led me to the likes (and liking) of Gertrude Stein, The New York School, the yet-to-be-classified Language Centered Poets, Kenneth Patchen and the so-called Avant Garde. My contemporaries in the MFA Program were young poets trying desperately, like me, to establish a foundation strong enough to support a lifetime commitment to the nebulous and cloudy persona of 'poet.' Some did and some didn't.

I also began to correspond with (and to) numerous and infamous poets that began to pass through the covers of the GEGENSCHEIN QUARTERLY. GEGENSCHEIN, begun in 1971 at Washington State University as a way to see myself in print, was becoming both a tangible, solid verification of the abstract notion of poetry (as something that could be 'literally' handed to someone) and as a statement of my developing poetics which in 1972 was that "human beings, not printing presses, wrote poetry." This idea came to life with the 'real' poets and the 'real' lives that inevitably crossed over into my 'real' life.

The form of my content (and discontent) gradually emerged from my first attempt at poetics which simply saw a poem as a combination of traditional, logical patterns on one side, and sporadically, out of nowhere, illogical abstractions on the other. These "I" lands of imagination represented the disparate, universal events that occur simultaneously with my own present (which I called SHRAPNELISM). My new way of saying the same thing was a process of fragmentation of a different kind, mirroring the center of an explosion, rather than the periphery. I ran and hid in the language. I played hide and seek within the confines of definition. My real life was exploding from within, sending torrential waves of motion to the shores of my consciousness while the emotion in my poems could be found in the bumping of definition, the criss-crossing of sounds and the simultaneous crashes of separate events.

IIIIIIIIIIIIIIIIIIIIIIIII
LLLLLLLLLLLLLLLLLLLLLLLLL
OOOOOOOOOOOOOOOOOOOOOOOOO
OOOOOOOOOOOOOOOOOOOOOOOOO
KKKKKKKKKKKKKKKKKKKKKKKKK
EEEEEEEEEEEEEEEEEEEEEEEEE
DDDDDDDDDDDDDDDDDDDDDDDDD
AAAAAAAAAAAAAAAAAAAAAAAAA
TTTTTTTTTTTTTTTTTTTTTTTTT
MMMMMMMMMMMMMMMMMMMMMMMMM
YYYYYYYYYYYYYYYYYYYYYYYYY
AAAAAAAAAAAAAAAAAAAAAAAAA
RRRRRRRRRRRRRRRRRRRRRRRRR
MMMMMMMMMMMMMMMMMMMMMMMMM

&&&&&&&&&&&&&&&&&&&&&&&&&

iiiiiiiiiiiiiiiiiiiiiiiii
ttttttttttttttttttttttttt
wwwwwwwwwwwwwwwwwwwwwwwww
aaaaaaaaaaaaaaaaaaaaaaaaa
sssssssssssssssssssssssss
nnnnnnnnnnnnnnnnnnnnnnnnn
'''''''''''''''''''''''''
ttttttttttttttttttttttttt
mmmmmmmmmmmmmmmmmmmmmmmmm
yyyyyyyyyyyyyyyyyyyyyyyyy
aaaaaaaaaaaaaaaaaaaaaaaaa
rrrrrrrrrrrrrrrrrrrrrrrrr
mmmmmmmmmmmmmmmmmmmmmmmmm

what used interrogatively as a request for specific information used interrogatively to inquire about the character, occupation, etc., of a person used interrogatively to inquire as to the origin, identity, etc., of something used interrogatively to inquire as to the worth, usefulness, force, or importance of something used interrogatively to request a repetition of words or information not fully understood, usually used in elliptical constructions used interrogatively to inquire the reason or purpose of something, usually used in elliptical constructions used relatively to indicate that which used in parenthetic clauses used to indicate more to follow, additional possibilities, alternatives, etc., used as an intensifier in exclamatory phrases, often followed by an indefinite article *do* to perform to execute to accomplish; finish; complete to put forth; exert to be the cause of; bring about; effect to render give or pay to deal with fix clean arrange move etc., (anything) as the case may require to travel traverse to serve suffice for to travel at the rate of (a specified speed) to make or prepare to serve a term in office or in prison to create form or bring into being to translate into or change the form of language of to study or work at or in the field of to explore or travel through as a sightseer to wear out; exhaust; tire to cheat trick or take advantage of to act or conduct oneself behave be in action to proceed to get along fare manage to be as to health to serve or be satisfactory as for the purpose suffice be enough to finish or be finished to happen transpire take place used without special meaning in interrogative negative and inverted constructions in imperatives with you or thou expressed and occasionally as a metrical expedient in verse used to lend emphasis to a principal verb used to avoid repetition of a verb or full verb expressing *these* plural of this *words* a unit of language consisting of one or more spoken sounds or their written representation that can stand as a complete utterance or can be separated from their elements that accompany it in an utterance by other such units words are composed of one or more morphemes with relative freedom to enter into syntactic constructions and are either the smallest units susceptible of independent use or consist of two or three such units combined under certain linking conditions as with the loss of primary accent which distinguishes black bird from black bird words are typically thought of as representing an indivisible concept action or feeling or as having a single referent are usually separated by spaces in writing and are distinguished phonologically as by accent in many languages speech talk especially insincere or vacuous the text or lyrics of a song as distinguished from the music contentious or angry speech a quarrel a short talk or conversation an expression or utterance warrant assurance or promise news tidings information a verbal signal as a password watchword or countersign an authoritative utterance or command *mean* to have in mind as one's purpose or intention intend to intend for a particular purpose destination etc., to intend to express or indicate to have as its sense or signification signify to bring cause or produce as a result to have (certain intentions) toward a person to have the value of assume the importance of to be minded or disposed have intentions ?

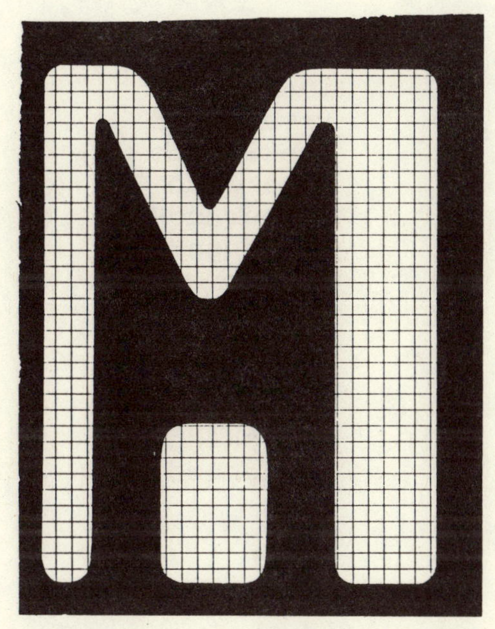

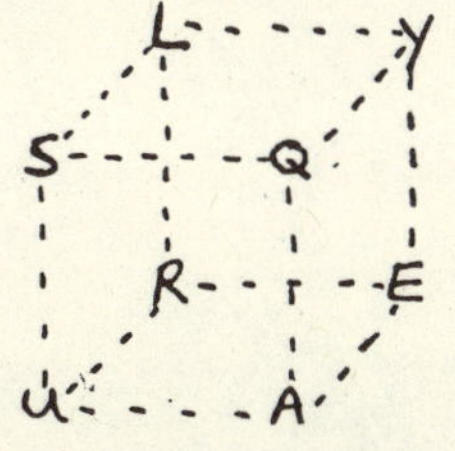
L
Y
S
Q
R
E
U
A

TheBoxAllo
wedItselfF
iveAlterna
tivesWhich
TookSixLea
pYearsToDi
scoverAndR
earrangeTo
FitItsSche
duleWhichH
adAlreadyC
alledForAS
eriesOfInt
erlockingC
irclesAndT

heirCircum
locutiousT
hrustThrou
ghHallowee
nEmptySuck
AndDeepAct
ualityWhic
hOccurredI
nTheCorner
sAndDrifte
dTowardsTh
eCenterWhi
chSurround
edItselfUp

AndBehindT
heDepthOfI
maginaryCu
besTheFlat
SquareImag
inedInGrea
tDepthToBe
TheUltimat
eRelations
hipTheUlti
mateForIts
ShallowSin
gularityDo
wnThroughH
istoryAndB

ackBeyondT
heGoblinsS
kinWhichLi
esDeeplyFl
atAgainstT
heClocksFa
ceHangingF
latAgainst
TheCurvesO
fSpaceAndI
tsEverendi
ngSpectrum

Thi
sWa
sTh
eFi
rst
Par
all
elD
raw
nFo
rGe
ome
try
&Actualit
yPerpendi
cularToIt

TheBoxWasAi
rToTheUnive
rseAWomanBl
ewHerLidAnd
CameForward

NowTheBoxCa
rsHitTheTra
ckAndRamble
Furthermore

SCHNEID

schlock
schmaltz

the par/snip caper rollicked, besides the maverick, who, in case that, granting or supposing that, on condition that, asked, would gull exponents coherently and femininity. In the period before the decision or conclusion of the penetralian lucky, we will have no further, upon request, of certainly, definitely, tribute paid to these goons as long since, provided that, I am in. And (used to connect grammatically coordinate words, phrases, or clauses) with; along with; together with; added to; in addition to; besides; also; moreover: PENS AND PENCILS/Or (used to correct or rephrase what was previously said):

HIS AUTOBIOGRAPHY, OR RATHER, MEMOIRS, IS READY FOR PUBLICATION,

rather, out.

PARABIOSIS

A
Q P
P
Q
F
X X
Q
P
B

an old legend:

PQ is always equal to PF, and focus on the scrambled cones both existing and imagined by a common parabola. By order of the Directrix, XX must be maintained as the axis and is. LIKE WOW, putting aside, the plane curve intersects, like is a parabole and equidistant, by comparison this is parabolic and parabolic.

the moral: WHETHER YOU ARE A MATH MAJOR OR AN ENGLISH MAJOR, AND ASSUMING YOU REALLY KNOW YOUR SHIT, YOU STILL DO NOT KNOW THE COMPLETE STORY.

A SHOWER OF AFFECTION

Principally the washcloth in the closet.
Wooly calves and women's liberation.
The Schick personna sweats and groans.
Principally the washcloth in the closet.

January freezes in these tracks.
Cubes of porcelain scrub against the curb.
Clean sheets wear pastel jackets.
January freezes in these tracks.

The air jet lifts its cold pucker.
Pop tarts jump into the sky.
The tub is clogged with brooms.
The air jet lifts its cold pucker.

The rain hops down on stilts.
A voice sinks into soiled bibs.
The toilet circles over drowned eagles.
The rain hops down on stilts.

The mud slides into my veins.
Knives attack the napkin.
Fuck me through the pistil!
The mud slides into my veins.

Quick get the mop!
Quick get the mop!
Quick get the mop!
Hand me the washcloth!

1 2 3 4 5 6
6 1 5 2 4 3
3 6 4 1 2 5
5 3 2 6 1 4
4 5 1 3 6 2
2 4 6 5 3 1
   5 3 1

vaseline
syzygy
wrangled
slides
the
strain

strain
vaseline
the
syzygy
slides
wrangled

wrangled
strain
slides
vaseline
syzygy
the

the
wrangled
syzygy
strain
vaseline
slides

slides
the
vaseline
wrangled
strain
syzygy

syzygy
slides
strain
the
wrangled
vaseline

the
wrangled
vaseline

You Don't Know Me Phil Demise

COMMUNICATION

telephone wires are for the birds
found them outstanding
found them out
found them out aloft

found them outstanding
stiff winter commas
found them out aloft
shaking the wind in the

stiff winter commas
kkkkkkkkkkkkkkkkkkk
shaking the wind in the
wind up with wings with

kkkkkkkkkkkkkkkkkkk
stretch raise the voice
wind up with wings with
wire teeth the the

stretch raise the voice
they fly off of off
wire teeth the the
taut to speak to bend

they fly off of off
found them out aloft
taut to speak to bend
found them outstanding

FRIDAY IN VIRGINIA, EDT.

i(n)t ended

on we

french/cupcakes/cancer

incisor/bi cuspis/molar/wisdom/and a thumb

Come Come

Come
this disturbance
K-os undoubtedly
belongs

happy and many
happy returns

BEGGING
BEGINNING

THIS IS A FOLLOW THE NUMBERS

nn
(make your own co~~rr~~ections)

continuous
no matter
what/what

AFTER WCW WS

in a "name"
                    an "n" and "a" "me"
noun and forever
                              stands
                              moniker
                              agnomen
                              apostrophe
hey rose!
              she she she not she
              the thing *in* she hears

they they they not they
the things in them

PLEGIA

*

bogged, and further.
The searching

and if it goes, so?
Comrades with spikes

,spoken behind gates.
And the glass is

-and it is-te tum!
fogged in fog

O brother,
Sigh.

*

1972
1970 also

*

place called place
and 1967 too

-noia,

para- nous -ia
far- too -factual

par.

rotsberpawn

roots
beer
    erb
    oops
soap
be
    wart
    oats
awn
ats
    as
    an
a
a

AN OLD FLAME

the light is returning
an arc, 2x2
spilling into its own
cups

and the source
capturing the downpour

a dislocated pinpoint
flashing in the brightness
hardly seen
as a soft retreat

a charge of loud light
neglected and muffled
by the circumstance,
by the protraction,
the circumference
of 2 perpendiculars
running parallel
to the Race

exhausted umbrellas
collapsing
in the high winds

broken springs
falling into
the solstice

coming back
with its reflection

a glimpse of purpose
circling the dead space

returning to my body
2x2
like a light rain

22°

COME TO THE CASBAH

"It's open to interpretation"

A box in a circle
Just flew overhead.
"Hello"

Box in a circle.
The divergent roads.
Main Street.
The wood.
The rules.
The ever increasing
Toads.

"Well I'll be..."

MAY I HAVE THIS...

1.

A job is a paper bag.
Air makes a cup.
January stayed up all night.

"Artificially"

Dance. Dance. Dance.

2.

Separate

The
legs.

"Simultaneously."

FIVE OR SIX THINGS TO EAT DURING THE FUEL CRISIS

1.

"If it is Art it cannot be understood by everyone"

2.

folding chairs
a juke box
cups and saucers
winter
a wax museum

TO COUNT ON ME YOU MUST HAVE MY NUMBER

1.

"The sky is no longer just."

(space)

Around the corner.

2.

He says: I see it clearly"
The parrot says: I see it clearly"
The echo says: I see it clearly, too"

CHEEK IN TONGUE

1.

"And finally..."

blue
re
moved
its
wind

stark naked red.

"The echo heard its own voice."

Talk,
It was a parrot

"unquestionably a remark."

2.

Hold your horses.

"You'll make an impression"

PUNTO *(el espanol roto)*

como porque cualquier un zapato despues azul desperado
tal vez un zapato en un llamo bonito
por despues de mayo y mas de diciembre

otra vez lo pregunta rojo y verde tu
para para en una pared y un automovil
porque lo dijo pero lo dijo fue a luna

y entonces el mundo viene en blanco negro
y entonces antes de bailar por un perdiendo
y entonces yo deseo ser en mi casa invierno

THEY THE TWO
a comma

CHAPTERS:

one two three four five six seven eight nine ten,

CHAPTER ONE.

this is the first sentence of the story

what will happen when the voice gives
and how will you know and through what

but my eyes are a weird size
when they are closed

occasionally he said occasionally
and then played with his mustache

there is no third person

she said she said
i don't know where i fit in

they held tightly

CHAPTER TWO.

there is laughter

a red silence relentless
spreading yes spreading all over

it is hidden

it is loud she said
he said it is loud

they whisper

CHAPTER THREE.

when i tell you it ends

you mean it's over
right through the red

no when i tell you it ends

no comma when i tell you comma
it ends

CHAPTER FOUR.

just for your information

period two days late
three days early period

i knew the explosion would come he said

he knew the explosion would come she said
she knew he knew but period

guess who i am the third person

but you said
they said period

CHAPTER FIVE.

nothing permanent burned

it is permanent it is
i hope she said

he is i thought

i am i think
but certainly

as i am they said

CHAPTER SIX.

off the chest

good now let's do it
all over the hill

she dreamed yes i said

but let's smile okay he said
i'll grab your hand ready

they the strand

CHAPTER SEVEN.

after that back to back

and out he said out
of in and into out

just like that

they the two drip
up the sprout

CHAPTER EIGHT.

who did you see today

with my eyes closed
i could count them on one hand

she said who

he said i could count them
she said he could shove them

they said it didn't move them

CHAPTER NINE.

the bedroom is a factor

and i think so too she said
it most certainly is and now

i will dress up and then down

and me i will come
and watch
you will he said

and i will moan in your ear they said

CHAPTER TEN.

they the two smile

wave goodbye until next
i said and twirled to the band

and a one and a two and a

this is the last and final word
comma

,

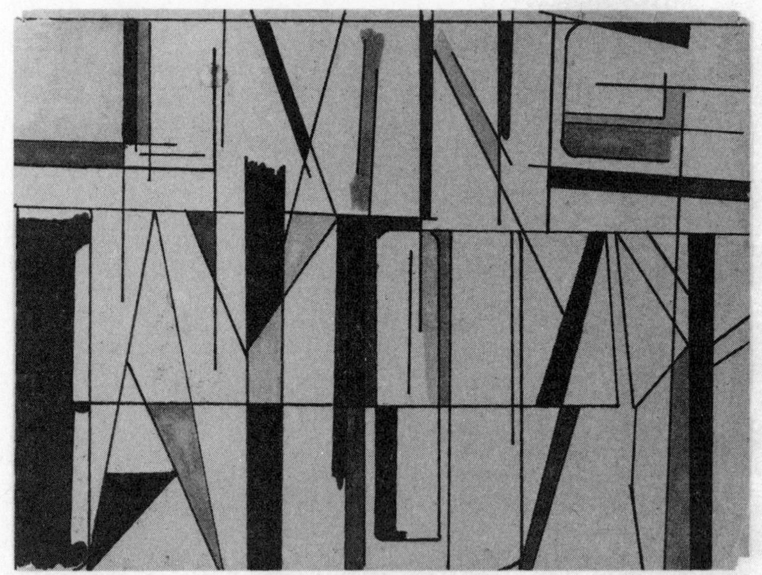

Living Day Today Phil Demise

an

A

A PART A

I
am
to
write
a
over
and
over
a
over
a
long
over
a
poem
go
on
over
a
over
and
a
fine
go
a
head
go
on
over
a
go
a
long
a
go
on

like
as
is
all
most
all
is
as
a

ie
as
dumb
as
a

there
a
tall
order
at
all
order
there
is
a
but
on
and
is
gone
as
a
over
a
go
is
as
gone
as
no

44°

no
and
so
on
a

where
a
go
there
and
here
go
there
for
a
ware
like
their
gun
and
snug
as
a

come
on
a

come
on
a

a
is
as
at
om
or
a
gain

45°

like
spl
it
is

a
pro
pos
as
is
a
gate
and
as
long
as
you
are
in
a

a
drift
like
as

a
droit
like
is

an
a
is
a
a
as
like
is
an
as

46°

a
id
is

and
first
of
all
a
is
a
skew
long
gone
and
on
poem
for
got
in
a
line

a
bra
ca
dab
ra
a
pear
a
please
please
a
plea
as
apple

47°

a
bun
dance
in
a
bout

a
is
a
way
out
a
far
with
out
a
way
in

a
vowel

allow
a
low
view
a
a
round
an
aura
an
a

are
is
a
we
verb
in

48°

an
act
of
a

be
causes
a
be
comes
a
be
cause
a
over
a
be
gun
a

an
order
be
gins
in
a
flash
as
a
on
an
a
an
other

as
an
a
goes
so
goes

49°

an
other

a
like
an
a

just
a

like
a
id
like
a

a
float
and
wide
in
a

a
way
in

abecedarian — a beginner

ab esse — absent

ab extra — from the outside

aborad	away from the mouth
about	of
absolute	perfect

abusage	wrong words
abut	touch edge
acalculia	no numbers

acaroid	resembling tick
acaudal	tailless
accipiter	hawk

achech	winged lion
acciaccatura	crushing grace
achilary	no lip

acicula	needlelike crystal
ack ack	gun fire
acouasm	hissing hallucination

adunc	curved inward
advection	movement of air horizontally

A bomb *See* atomic bomb

acarpous barren
accouchement gestation
accouterment trappings

absterge	purge
abulia	impaired volition

achalasis	tight gut
acockbill	pointed up
a couvert	under cover

acronychous	having claws
acutilingual	a sharp tongue
ad captandum vulgus	to please the mob

Adonai	God
Allah	God
ad quem	to which

adularescent	milky bluish luster
ad patres	dead

afghanets	gusty dust bearing wind
afflatus	inspiration

65°

alewife	a North American fish
alewife	barmaid

allision — crashing ships
aliped — like bat's toes
alis volat propriis — she flies with her own wings

ala — a wing
ajiva — without life

F
U
C
K
I
N
G

A

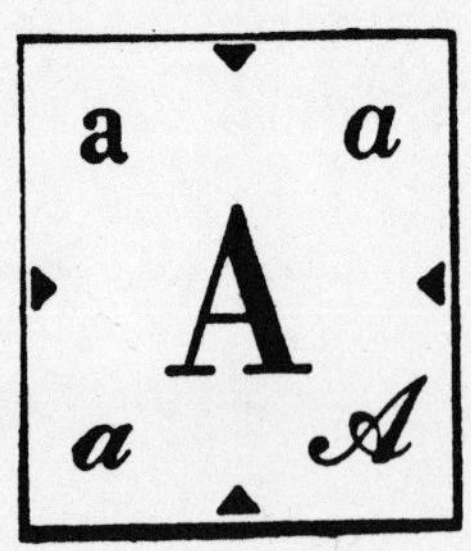

69°

potty donor and fried legs, perhaps shoddy tubes will suit you more often..."That's it!" Rancor exclaimed and gave it up to the heavens like fish. Pike ran hurriedly for permission fron Ann Blyth and returned empty faced with cupcake fingertips and duzzed overalls. "Where you been Pike?" Nona sent through the mails. Two weeks later nothing was there.

in the same place, elsewhere. Regular Lewis had a ping pong aura running clearly up and down his negative. His blood turned the color of paranoia and spelling, alternately. "You're a chocolate mess!" his children would greet him at the door, the back door, and kiss his knobs over and over again. A little later Regular died when he bit into a thumbnail sketch.

"You've got to stop biting if you ever want to live again," they said to his window. Glaucoma burst in without eating dinner, screaming at the top of her chest, "Rapidamente faster por favor please senor sir ahora now." "Forever jelly," the window breathed closed.

vaht ish dish jibberish? Clown dropped his cheeks sadly. "Pick them up," Balls pleaded. "Get on your knees if necessary." Clown had Lion lick his face and put it in a cannon. "There I go," Clown boomed.

Pandemonium has some body.

if no if ands or buts but what if and/or buts in if and when no if ands or buts are, then what? Jezzebell plunked down a five spot and got undressed in two months. Dr. punched the two way mirror with both fists. "Commitment," he begged. Without any formal introduction their lungs collapsed just like in an opera. No two ways about it.

"Would you believe it," he said, "the moment I say anything, it changes. It seems that circumstance has a mind of its own, separate from the appearance of reality. A very warped mind at that."

He turned away only to become a fat man. I watched his flesh grow wide with gray moisture and suddenly he became the sky.

THE MAKING OF
THE BODY POLITIC 1973
an innerview

relative to the
from which side

doggerel
why i never
besides

***

what is your
then
on

obviously

could you be

than
that

i am of the
and the that
they are wanted
but
then they are there
which needless
detracts

***

you have been as
saying
the
spoken
sucks

first let me
it was not said
which if
would
back
tongue
no
what is being
is not said
it was felt

how would
by
without it

can't
but
can

***

now
like to
to another
if i

certainly

been seen
on numerous
without
could you

no image
imagine

***

and lastly
what
to do with
the rest
and
with whom
do you expect

based on
and the call
i'm quite
that will
the course
naturally she
but in no way
in the way of
by the way of
or of the way of
in conclusion

E PLETHORA UMBRA

i stand between two mirrors

i see my being become
a wing of bodies
passing through the sun

i ask myself
which one?   which one?

GBBG

,first paragraph

Adios, the plaque denunciates. O wooster, unfurnished flats, unfinished, unjust flats, overstuffed lulls, full of campus, adios, No etc., dull mountains, beer, cloisters, and no etc. Suffering proof, huddled in claps, proof of slack, of necessity for pillows, slouched like hills, pins suffering proof. Oblong shifts, oxygen, language centered medulla, mad caps, and brains commingle like a landscape, and all that space in air obsessed with catalysts and intellects, subtitles, reptilia, poofs, and like magic, oblong shifts.

,tenth line

Linkage, perhaps, clank in the lounge, a deep addic.
O no, no clinker, o no.

,ragraph

Paralyze, sort of, bolic, and tender boredom and bygones. I watch the sheets of brass. I watch the shade recede and all the tongues twist into rough winds, punching bags, and paralyzed fists swallowing margins, style, and sheets, all lists reduced to green rules, gainfully employed, paralyzed.

,paraadios, bye bye, bowling pins

O

god w
illin
g i w
ill g

the sky
is not
the limit
is it?

and
dna

81°

We live in the oblivion of our metamorphoses

Paul Eluard

Herm Freeman

subLETTERS
Summer/Fall 1974
New York City

subLETTERS - Summer/Fall 1974

R & I finally had to leave the womb. We had lived on the edge within the soft confines of academia for 3 years and now we had to continue on with our 'life sentence.' Not that this academic pause and the criss-crossings of personal fantasies hadn't left their scars. They had. Our relationship to everything had been changed and my own confidence had been pulled in two directions, leaving it limp and vulnerable. We headed back home to New York City where just three years before I had left in a state of wonder. Now I was returning with a degree of fluff (MFA) and uncertainty.

This period was one of adjustment and pain. I first had to adjust to being an abstraction (a poet) in a city of concretions. Just living was not enough. Someone had to go out and 'make' a living. New York City now stood as the other half of the romantic notion of 'living for' and 'as' your Art - it was the REAL half of the fantasy - no income with a dark outcome. As the metaphor for such heavy floatation and uncertainty, R & I began our return by subletting apartments - living within someone else's stability.

Our first sublet was in the sterile, white complacency of the upper east side of Manhatten which R & I shared with R.D., a poet, and his girlfriend, B.B., a painter. I felt uncomfortable to the point of silent desperation. I was still in 'academic-mode' which in this city was useless and untranslatable.

By the Fall of 1974 we had sublet our third apartment which was on East 22nd Street off Park Ave.. We were slowly edging downtown, closer to our 'element' and we were finally alone. R began to work 'temporary' jobs which was, at least, less transient than my position as 'poet.' We were, at best, grinding out a life with one foot still in the dream.

It was at this point that my instincts for survival began to surface and I began to rethink a new shape that was to be my new definition. My points of reference began to include painters and painting and inklings of Futurism and Dada. The need for Manifesto, to declare my existence, was imminent.

It began with the NOWISM MAN INFESTO which tried, in a philosophical sense, to tie together all the simultaneous and disparate impressions which were now a part of my aesthetic, which had become my life. I began to verbalize what my body already knew to be true, that a 'thing' and its opposite exist side by side, simultaneously and they are neither good nor bad. An ex-tension of this awareness blossomed into the TELEVISIONISM MANIFESTO which became my personal statement about 'value' and 'worth.' Trying desperately to find some value in 'reflection,' I declared that all things have an inherent 'worth' just for 'being' and their 'value' was merely what other individuals placed upon it (their opinion). This made all my work 'worth' doing even if it had no apparent 'value' at the time. It was a trick to keep myself going and it worked (and still does). I took all my negatives and positively distributed them throughout the city and my work.

Though I still remained 'in the language,' a new, conscious process began to appear. It was that of the 'list' - the vertical listing of simultaneous events and emotions as both a list of statements and a list of phrases separated by a pause (comma). I continued my natural opposition to the horizontal, syntactic flow of one emotion/event.

R & I were still struggling, though with slightly less discomfort, when we hit the JACKPOT! (a T.V. quiz show on NBC where R appeared and won $1500, a Crock Pot and a year's supply of Rice-a-Roni). We finally had a little nestegg to crack open and we once again took up the search for the 'living' dream.

bioillogical

physioillogical

neuroillogical

HOMELESS REPRESENTATION

living day today
"I left my wallet in NYC"
and dance
never take no for
an ecliptic cadence
caught in the act

almost mostly
preinscribed *blanc*
static cutoff clowns

the here and now
and again hovering
if you want an audience
crowds of blues and greens
a wind gusto

avoid eye contact
behind the canvas
ends and odds
deep in the epistle
knifeshots

skipping artifacts
a hesitant urgency
and an orange

LIVING COLOR

pliable as silver rivers
pliable as gun shot sounds
pliable as line breaks

soft as up and up
soft as pliable
soft as soft its ffft

standing as standing
standing as sitting
standing as running

as as human slinky
as as present proper
as as as

as blue as

FAT PRIDE

1. the honesty kick is sucking furiously
2. the picnic divulged, apparently graphic
3. the boston spilled a victim forbidden in
4. the door, a telephone, and a bed, consistency
5. sassy movietales show ears as private and naughty
6. turn the phenomenon of excess around themselves
7. the vacuum and the dust cleansing the windex
8. the windex turning in its commercial for glass
9. the honesty kick is sucking furiously

CONTRA DICTIONS

I'm sitting on the floor in a chair.
I'm running along the walk.
I'm waking up in my sleep.
The blue dish is green.
My dreams take place before my eyes.
Nobody wants me can have me.
Bills mount and multiply like bulls and cows.

IMPROMPTU ENERGY CRISIS

short
purple decrease in shirt sleeves

tall
fabricated sufficient order

fat
dilapidated cold and chance

thin
split and jerky line

high
diamond white energy

low
deep intrusion of fact in point

form
from the law of the letter

content
with the outcome of cow

TEN WAYS OF LOOKING AT A BLANK SLATE

Answers to the octagon are hidden
by the hubcaps snapped from hoodlums.

You are the partaker in every theft
including the language from my mouth.

Some geese can spell backwards if
their wings are set at 90° north.

Flocking to the top they oversee
their mark in a rearview beak.

You have stolen three directions
and one demented sleep from their tales.

Take those conjunctions from your tongue!
You stupid child, you will die someday!

What do we have down here but a notion
trapped in a capsule of ice?

We have toothpicks, jets, petunias, tissues,
charity, laundry, wallets, and octagons.

NO CIGAR (as in Close But)

a smidgeon of matter surrounded by thirteen blue boys
painted by an imposter

"something will turn up as long as you avoid the vegetable"

twenty routines are taken aback and whisper through the
fade out out out out out out out out out out out out out
out out long candle and the drenched shirt, simply because

the fabrication fits the raincoat
the nullification drapes the judgment

no matter, a smidgeon, so what

someday the withdrawal will be complete and leave no
balance," no cigar, no body,

the just space we are thrown into, no matter, no water

remains, no, no remains, just space, so what

no cigar, close but

MUSE um

et al geosyncline und graywacke,

the difference being twenty thousand leagues
plus
internal communication with goose bumps under foot,

paraperfect in the child part of being ongoing

adulting the sweet barf of prehistory with shellack
covering fascination like an armoured dinosaur

out of the magnificence of time

the ho hum parody of sounds close my ears
shun all kinds of music surrounding boredom

out of the magnificence of time

priapic figurines

$4:45
no no

kick if
and and

but

in

izzat
gisant

guzzle little bugger, the gunk is freely espoused finally, dice
fossick fossick
fossick fossick

nepenthe

THE SPACE IN PAUSE

In the wherever , perhaps now , the ultra violet
alacrity and viscous attachment beneath the
surface of our systems ,
may rise in the split second , comb the jungles of
excitement, but whatever , since the confusion
has turned into birds.

The show off showed up, thrusting panels of
discussion, free ways of wheeling poking through
his chest, sucking in with all
his might his might his fantastic strength, with authority,
his creation, up to the whims, the spinning white
eyeballs.

All things considered. ,

SURPRISE

uprise
here,
from, away, this barren fertility,
up up
christ, my wrist and its action, jerks
you know,
witches,
spasm, up front, windshieldless, crashing shrinkage,

now is later
uh oh,
full of two months following
this is it
untotally, and committed
of preposition, of before, of at,
of after,
the plotz, the new carnation, pajamas,
,off

CORPSE MUSCLE

tripping into succumb
the color of bulbous blood
the soft bash
the memoirs of the future
the bell ticking in my wrist
expectations breathing
the after birth strangulation
an accomplishment
like death to keep you going

SLEEPING, I AM PRONE TO LIE

The best stance for fucking is circum.
Whereby navigation roundly begins.
The Cape of Big Wheels was anticipated.

To begin with 'to begin' and go from there.
Around the Horn of Bungle and up yours.
Look. A circus is your cup of tea.
Look again. It is pink.

Don't expect a crowd.

SHE SHELLS

I am retiring.
Retrograde pistols give me backward wounds.
I put Shelley to my ears.
I hear oceans not saying a word.
A woman sits on my zero.
It becomes oblong and eggish.

It means nothing.

THE GREEN BLASTULA

on his return from deep aggravation
a wiry silence sits in the anticipated cup
where the moving lips perch and flap like gloves
in fact they are gloves and they do flap bye bye
to his wiry eyes while he sleeps in his body

on boy he says to the after taste gurgling
like a mountain's climax
oh boy he says to the hole in his sock

the excuse that is given is tangled down
in the galaxy's tentatives and shines as bright
as six white horses coming around the snowcaps
but it is really tucked away in a dream that sleeps
in a dream and is kissed on the forehead
by a pair of white gloves

on his return from the pounding water
the fresh silver dripping from his hair
reminds him of the inconsequence of disappearance
and the sequence of deep aggravation
moving in formation from ice white to invisible white
to incredible red to the fresh silver
dripping from his hair

Herm Freeman

IMPRACTIBLE JOKES

He is a big prank. Gotten to the point
he can't even differentiate between.
And you know what that means. Check your
coat. He can oddly differentiate 9 & 55
but what good does that do? He must pull
gags so that his windpipe doesn't starve.
Usually, once they're pulled off, he uses
them for gloves. He must always remember
not to leave fingerprints but an entire
finger here and there is okay....even this
is a diversion....better watch your wallet!

There's nothing like a good sneak before dinner.

MOLECULAR POOF

Daddy's falling.
Blue anchors sink in my stomach.
You have my deepest conveyance.
The energy dance ceased.
The dance has become distance.
My brain is nauseous.
A boulder grows beneath my hair.
I love poached eggs.
The condition calls for action.
I believe in privacy.

RED SOME, LOSE SOME

Now my thoughts are red. Remaining tracks
Can be petunias in the road bed. Along the
Rib cage, night spikes my lungs with sleep.
I have caved in! Hard hats split the revenge.
White corpuscles swim upblood to meet a
Torn cartilage and a weeping muscle. To warn
Them. Impending coal. Industrialization.
Representation. And finally, blessed
Decomposition makes all things grow again
Upside down.

NOWISM MAN INFESTO

I declare:

1. help me little god, things are first nature to me

2. things are not good and good

3. things are the subject of art, emotion is the movement of things

4. things grow inside out, emotion gets crowded, grows inside in

5. a situation is a thing

6. emotion is no thing, it is the speed of change

7. no thing is not nothing, it is pure light, the no movement of no thing

8. no movement is all movement at once

9. nothing is space where things and no things coincide

Things are the color and shape of paint, the sound and meaning of words. No thing is the form, the movement of things, the no movement of all movement at once. Impossibility is all things at once, no thing, nothing.

10. talent is a sensibility, not a craft

11. craft is a border line, a vertical, a pole around which talent rallies and spirals

12. talent does not rely on craft, it rallies and spirals

13. talent is creation, craft is the medium

14. the medium is that which is between the artist and the observer, the language

15. art is a personality, a noncommunicative beast, that is, unable to speak, but when observed, a presence comes to mind

nyc 1974

NOWISTIC

It's friday again
and it's tuesday
people breakdown then
Ah what the
The orange juice is coffee
by now it's a package
out for social obligations
It's all the same
out the window
The shadow

when monday snowed
The french bullet
The hard and hilarious
smell of arithmetic

of cheap appearances
victory over the sun
The blue clear decrease
The window

How it came about
how what snow?
They say backwards purple
in jumpy
explodes with extra effervescence

It's my dopey modes
to return yellowy up
Forget deep purple, manny, joy

The untested

to kill an elephant
The chihuahua cry
inside
doubled over
informed crescently
and this is my way
under
under any circumstances
The great cut

a list of unheard
blue in its vertical
A tagged up advance
and the clearest sort of night

Of fragmental
across a napping 8
out and scored
Becauses like a dream

ABOUT TRADITION AND THE YANKEES VERSES CLEVELAND

The ex tilted foreplay
yanked triple decked out
In in, see see, curved
and this is the killer
at the fence the ball died

And Vital Blue
plays for the white angels

get this

cleverly

, Unsigned

Sometimes it comes in
clear as a bell
A busily hued cartoon
and the bouncing ball
Derived from angles
transversing an eclipse
The tries and tribulations
and all the laughing
The total medium belly

and sliding
sliding
It is sliding
arrived and

in the flag
move slightly off
Began

After WATCHING ROBIN MAKE HER FIRST CAR OUT OF TUNE NECESSITY, untitled

BLOOMINGDALES

The trees this fall
are the trees
Have bricks?
It is one inside one
cups and stacks of cups
and pigments
The not there cue
Oh and
Bits and tids
as if the bouncing process
Lands in low snowdrops
in over sneezing jowls
The pinstriped overalls

It is under heads
the dead Christmas rush
the autonomous bitch
Closing in

Are the trees this fall
the trees?
Have bricks
bulging at the certainty
of clothes
Those peachy colors flaming
and the corporate soft juice
the buy and buy come on
of the good life crumbs
Took off blizzardly
like a slant of minstrel
The scratch of magic markers
careless stubbing and
rejection
Take brown ink send red ink
The time of slaps is passed
unlististic joke
And wave bye bye
kooky civilization

TELEVISIONISM MANIFESTO #ONE

1. Anything can and will happen.
2. Well.
3. Well.
4. I am alone and I am not alone.
5. My Art is not separate from my Self but Fame is.
6. Nothing can be Made to happen but in Making, things happen.
7. Whatever happens happens.
8. The Future is Unknown.
9. The Past is Known.
10. The Present is Knowing Nothing.
11. There is no rush to Do because not Doing Is Doing.
12. I need not convince Anyone of Anything.
13. I am Good at what I Do.
14. There is no such thing as Best.
15. Success is Failure and Failure is Success.
16. Value is a Matter of Opinion.
17. Value is not Worth.
18. All States of Mind are Temporary.
19. Dream Life is Vertical.
20. Real Life is Horizontal.
21. Explanations are a waste of Time.
22. Standing Under is Understanding.
23. We Stand Under all that IS and WILL BE.
24. We are Above all that WAS.
25. What I am DOING IS important.
26. To be On Top of Things is a False Perspective.
27. To be Above It All is a False Perspective.
28. To think OF is not to think ABOUT.
29. My LIFE (Dream Life + Real Life) is a List of lists.
30. Language is a Brain with No Body.
31. Art is a Brain with No Body.
32. What I say is what I am when I am saying IT.
33. Addition is the Highest Form of Knowledge.
34. Addition is Subtraction, Division, and Multiplication.
35. A Lie is not False.
36. A Lie is the Altered Ego of Truth.

37. Art is not Truth which is Truth.
38. Laughter is the Realization that a Lie is Pleasure.
39. Pleasure is Really Unreal.
40. Worth is inherent in all things Real and Unreal.
41. Value is Worth in relation to one's own possibilities and is a Lie.
42. Is forty too.
43. Disappointment is an Addition that is Subtraction.
44. What IS Done is a particle of what you are Doing.
45. What is not Done is a particle of what you will be Doing.
46. IS DOING is the Vertical Axis of ALL LIFE and ALL ART.
47. Anything that comes to Mind IS DOING and WILL BE DONE.
48. Dream Life runs counter (Vertical) to The Programmatical System which is Real Life (Horizontal).
49. The result is Opposition and Frustration and Being, rubbed the wrong way.
50. IS fifty.
51. Fiction is the Opposite of Friction.
52. Worry is a Horizontal slamming into a Vertical.
53. When two Horizontals meet, a Horizontal Stasis is achieved.
54. Sleep and Death is an example of Horizontal Stasis.
55. When two Verticals meet, Ecstasis is achieved.
56. Art and Dreams is an example of Ecstasis.
57. Dream Life is a Fiction.
58. Real Life is a Friction.
59. SKELETON OF A DROOP.
60. with the greatest of disease, curiously.
61. brats, I am feeling no rush, no bullet.
62. a tail on the convicted brain, shake it, turn.
63. sincerely floating, tripping, flipping over.
64. disbulbous, flat things.
65. thin, the pinky of a dream, the width.
66. vocally, silently excavating.
67. who who, specifically, who who.
68. rising tormented sleeping pinched.
69. wisely undecided, clearly.

70. twisting string, unfolding memorable thickness.
71. petering spunk, going out.
72. I drip off my own energy like a Television tube.

TELEVISIONISTIC BRAIN DEATH DRAMA

Well?
Well? What?
Well I'm afaid I'm.
I'm.
Going?
I'm muscle.
Contraction?
M'I?
What I'm.
I'm I'm I.
I'm's.
It's a crime that I'm.
Scared.
Scar red?
Scarred.
SACRED.
The torpedo's eyes were momentarily depressed as the electricity was.
Delivered.
Tremble fish!
The brain discovering.
Uncovering?
The Brain.
An electric influence machine.
Scooping it out through the nostrils with a bent metal tool.
Built in distortions.
Brain Death!
Moving Parent?
I'm transparency.
Winky Dink?
Non thinking brain.
Where was cancer before there was Cancer?
Shoot wine into the blood.
Fermentation.
Irritability.
Animal Spirits leap into the fleshy fibres.
Not getting *away* with murder.
Bringing it to?

And I'm.
Afraid time won't tell?
That light lipped bitch!
Each different.
Each melts.
Too much to live for.
I'm.

Space into space
All is nowhere
Place of impalpable nuptials

Octavio Paz

Herm Freeman

MacDOUGAL STREET SUITE
Fall/Winter 1974
New York City

MacDOUGAL STREET SUITE - Fall/Winter 1974

On a quiet Sunday walk in Greenwich Village, R & I came upon a small, basement apartment for rent in a delightful brownstone on MacDougal Street off W. 3rd, on what was once the main drag of the beat generation. We had just received the money from R's T.V. adventure and we were anxious to settle in somewhere. When we contacted the owner of the building, he claimed (with authority) that Louisa May Alcott had actually lived and written in this brownstone. It was perfect. A 'gingerbread apartment' in the middle of (and slightly below) an enchanted history.

My life twisted, turned and finally broke in this miniature fable. The view out of our window was like comparing metaphors to metaphysics. It was from below 'see' level so that when I looked up I saw the bottom - the tires, the sidewalk and the feet of MacDougal Street's active life. Occasionally a 'tourist' would bend to peek in on us, hoping to catch a glimpse of 'bohemians' in their natural habitat. I would reciprocate and occasionally stand at our window and in the invisibility offered by being 'beneath' them, I would look up at the quick and private passings of *their* lives.

R continued to work temporary jobs and I got a part-time position in Bloomingdale's art supply and book department. By this time I had remade contact with my lifelong friend, H.F., a painter who had just returned from an academic experience at the University of Indiana. He was living in Westport, Connecticut, a one hour train ride which became my artistic lifeline.

H and I merged on our most primitive front: music. We got very stoned and we explored; H on keyboards and me on 'gutar', vocals and 'theory.' Our explorations took us further into the art of performance which was, coincidentally, New York's emerging art form. I began further and more intense inquiries into the Futurists, the

Dadaists, Erik Satie, John Cage and, in general, the open-ended theories of 'art as life' and 'sound as sound.' It was all music, all performance and all simultaneous. To represent our new definition, H & I gave ourselves a name, claiming title to our new characters - NOYES.

At the same time that I was dealing with such wide open spaces, I had to physically deal with the small enclosures of my real life which gave rise to another example of 'extreme simultaneity,' THE GREAT NOVEL AMERICAN, PERHAPS. In it I attempted to reconcile the oxymoronic 'vastness' of the smallest particle, the infinity of a box (T.V.) and the quickly changing tenses of the Present. Life and Art were quickly closing the gap. (My ultimate statement of this sensibility was when I awoke one morning and envisioned my apartment as a 'gallery of ready-mades' and proceeded to label and title the groupings including R who was sleeping and entitled "Naked Sleep Prone to Dream." In my mind, I opened the doors to our apartment and invited the public.)

Then, in the midst of this 'artsy-fog,' suddenly, Bowling Green and its academic immorality came crashing in once again. R came home with a black-eye, the result of a secret rendezvous with Bowling Green's ex-poet-in-residence and his frustrated attempt to continue his 'academic pursuit' of my wife. I broke up (and down), packed my only faithful love, Ezra, my chihuahua, and left. Period,

Rude Alteration Phil Demise

MacDOUGAL STREET SUITE

1. NOTHING IS

Nothing Is Ugly, It's The Only Thing That Is. Nothing Is Simple, It's The Only Thing That Is. Nothing Is True, It's The Only Thing That Is. Nothing Is Complete, It's The Only Thing That Is. Nothing Is Timeless, It's The Only Thing That Is. Nothing Is Contradictory, It's The Only Thing That Is. Nothing Is Finished, It's The Only Thing That Is. Nothing Is Important, It's The Only Thing That Is. Nothing Is Silent, It's The Only Thing That Is. Nothing Is Complete, It's The Only Thing That Is. Nothing Is Everything, It's The Only Thing That Is. Nothing Is Present, It's The Only Thing That Is. Nothing Is Ultimate, It's The Only Thing That Is. Nothing Is Art, It's The Only Thing That Is. No Thing Makes Sense, It's The Only Thing That Does Nothing Is The Only Thing That Is.

2. MacDOUGAL STREET

-for Robin

When we go on or into a train, plane, ship or bus that will take us somewhere, we call it going aboard. Lucy is able to read. Lucy can read. Lucy knows how to read. Lenny has a ball. Lenny has one ball. As we turn or flip the corner, page, or over we see new things and call it going ahead. Jack must write about how cold it is. Jack has to write about how cold it is. It is cold. Presently ongoing cold. When the sky is grey in winter, it is cold. When the grey sky is in winter, it is cold, and we call it winter. The kids are lined up to climb aboard the bus. The kids are lined up to get on the bus. When we go on or into a train, plane, ship or bus that will take us somewhere, we call it going aboard. You can't judge a book by its cover. You can't judge a book based on its cover. When we cover up something we call it a coverup. You can't cover a judge by a book. You can't cover a judge based on a book. Lucy is able to read. Lucy can read. Lucy knows how to read. Jack must write about how cold it is. Jack has to write about how cold it is.

When we live on or into a street, we call it home.

3. THIS AND THAT

Come down in the world slow flux several hundred yards through the testes like a good tubule. Could *this* be passed on? This, you know, used to indicate a person, thing, idea, state, event, time, remark, etc., as present, near, just mentioned or pointed out, supposed to be understood, or by way of emphasis: *This* is my hat. This, you know, used to indicate one of two or more persons, things etc., already mentioned, referring to the one nearer in place, time, or thought; opposed to *that*: *This* is Lisa and *that* is Amy. This, you know, used to indicate one of two or more persons, things etc., already mentioned, implying contrast or contradistinction; opposed to *that*: I'd take *that* instead of *this*. These people are my friends. This problem has worried me for a long time.

Friends are closely associated with proximity. *This* is nearly true. And *that* is nearly true too.

When the train gets lost in the tunnel, where is the station? If it is not lost, where is the station?

The tunnel is the station. *This* is nearly true.

Going backwards we find the present. Friends are closely associated with proximity. *This* is nearly true. And *that* is nearly true too. A testimony to the continuum of sperm, its simultaneous activity and its ultimate continuum in a new form which is the same form thinking itself new. *This* sperm and *that* egg, that oocytic globe suspended in the space of human galaxies, in the convoluted fallopian tube, convolution as the solution to large surface in a limited space, and BINGO! *this* is nearly true, *that* passing on is a function of existence.

The answer to *that* question is yes.

STILL IS

for Phyllis and Herm Freeman

were are

,

familiar blip unappeared quite certainly?

(for)

is was/was is (presently)

;

is (still motionless etc)

:is jumping still (impossible)

ism's

.

.

)isual(

.

,

is *as* always

JUST STONE

-for Octavio Paz

I

Water over dances curving roundabout ever. Star urgency eyelids prophecies waves overlapped decline wings sky. Densities fateful bird singing happiness disappearing birds hand. Singing building suspended mountains agate bays body leaping body body transparency.

Sound presences transparencies another magic among autumn. World city celebrated blood ivy assaulted divided peaches birds noon. Desires naked water dreams flames moon imagining dream. Singing water they long water water breast tree.

River going mountain ravine thoughts forehead shattered one dark. Memory living-rooms away base memory it over away. Daylight moment thunderstorm night shadows side. Alone ends down mirrors image roadway shadow moment. Bird afternoon *tezontle* clusters light scatter building onward arcades garment transparent.

Deer night reclined rain face Melusine Persephone them them cloud star sword blood then itself. Jade queen stone moon thorn pain sea dead vertigo plant life lightning-flash wound down harrowing basalt desert wheat-ear.

Away face days wall face calling name face instant centuries eyes. Moment dream intertwined dream night feature guts soul calendar. Capitals things forehead night skeleton deliberately eyes years horrors. Fan images floats threatenings midnight hullabaloo masked itself perfect time scatters itself roots me branches birds circulates time.

Nevertheless approaching back now fills vanishes.

Saltpetre razors indecipherable wounds flame water stone loins dust time without reflecting corridor point hand galleries erect. Axe fascinating condemned slender moon penetrates desolate roots friends rot precipice. Wound healing intellect reflecting transparency eye itself clarity. Armour burning sheets awakening broken shrieking myself over photographs. One broom duster bones hole eyes ago.

II

Pit time mother father daughter son depth death eyes life? Be life death moment revealing is is. Planning summers ago throat light me here lost me night tree wind somewhere me dawn already watch word see reef we Perote? Places circles rooms hair dressing rooms.

Seven women sons shriek dust spittle static another portion paradise touching pirated centuries kissed together invulnerable origins names soul being. Adrift foundering wounds rooms paper newspaper spring tree raining children singing submarines waves phosphoresces pictures carpets. Caverns them flight door meal shells conquer here in eat water.

Sacred world day born transparency open silences away penitentiaries fences spurs wars gown Society Cross crocodile country architect uniform Church teeth courses invisible masks man self.

Down darkly is man death alive.

Kiss flesh forth world wine water doors number chain master. Changed recognizing names words law reward him. Crime incest mirrors reflections bread ashes delirium sodomite carnation stoning grinds life hours time shit.

Flower silence heaven time movement corolla hour masks transparent being nothingness self names. Streets corridors staircases advancing face self me going river fingers fingers smiling head hands smiling orange. Changed enlaced descending space silence eye clouds out float green happens communicating.

Blinking moment suns eyelid murder sound man field howl Cassandra crying rising a life ruins beheld Moctezuma insomnia death longer inch hands throne Lincoln theatre moan gaze me silences devil anecdotes over noises frenzy sounds ferocity mouth torturer victim flames.

Flaming music firebrand touching fire flame is smoke torturer. Cry silence silence nothing men passing? Eyelid nothing time dying death gestures dying us life end end pulse mask face alien ours. Ours are are emptiness horror others' are others ourselves acts everybody's other others exist existence ever farther horizon for away all.

III

Thou see other us breadman sailor Paul collective born. Death midnight daybreak liquids death birth depth together ashes breathe earth act aroused. Hand days grows done daybreak day dawns John all. Dawn day night transformed beating night Ourselves intertwined.

Awaken face vision yours death fountain faces face presences. Cannot things dreams stones blood sang way decay forehead closed clothes separated stone resurrects.

Water over dances curving roundabout ever.

WRITINGS

lne

The restraint of spontaneity is delicious after the fact.
The strain of restraint is rewarding like holding it in, a
giver of more
time.
Deciding *on* the moment and once *in* it never giving it
a second thought.
Letting first nature become second nature.
What
needs to be said down, the need to be said which is smack
in the middle
of its own appearance, there.
Very heavy if and when it appears.
Very full of meaning when it drops in like holding it in,
that
icy hard splash of relief against the philosophical
cheeks
of some ass's real existence and the double fold
two fold
second
thought
that is of primary importance. It is just this
that makes a mockery of the whole pretense of pretense.
Writings is
writings
no matter how you look at it, grimaced, twelve toned, or
bare assed,
it comes up to its own presence,
cannot go beyond,
cannot go back, cannot stay still,
unless
it wants to,
on second thought, interterrestrial, interesting, tertiary
and always primordial in its incumbrance.
A blue snake.

The page is a field, the wind its fingers all interfaced, prefaced, the momentous decision, which time it will be done and let go.

What is the expression of this flickering interface? Retrospect is the mother of meaning. Unexpect is the other mother, meaning
it is
simply
meaning full and meaning less like brother and sister one after the other and before the other alternately like a television image popping all over the set,

never set down while it's on,
a fine example
of relativity and vision.

While we're on the subject of art and life,
let me point up
the significance of that simple conjunction,
that *and*
that space.

That very same space that justly connected and continues to connect these words in my head and conversely disjoins them again
at the same time in this field of windy fingers
shuffling through the choices like
everyday life and art,
that *and* that space and

doing anything is worth doing, Period.

A definitely and infinitely forgettable experience shoved into a pouch, committed to belly,
and finished off by some external
power,
maybe the glass of subway riders.

3hree

Tomorrow, possibly
I will get a canvas and paint
shadows.

Supper is of the utmost importance! Everything is pretense! And since this is a search, maybe tension is too late! And extension too too late!

In that moment between the moment before and the moment you decide.

the sun in an unspecified position is day.
the sun in an unspecified position is night.

Between two unspecified positions is their shadow.
This occurs every one second and
the next second or second second, primarily when
we are alive.
Have you ever experienced such pretense!?
Forgetting is a thrust,
a contraction, a thrust.

News is old.

An aerial shot of existence will show it to be a dance,
elaborate,
mobile,
disjointed,
jerky,
discontinuous,
muscular, coupled, unnarrative, inaudible, articulate, simple,
gentle,
symmetric,
unavoidable,
beat,
playing its brains out
Or something like that but different.
Rock & Roll.

GREAT NOVEL AMERICAN PERHAPS

PREAMBLE

This is a beginning of a writing. It stars some person whose name hasn't come to me yet but I know it well. It takes place during several days in a week that somehow wanders all over the universe which narrows it down to sometime indefinitely. There is a city somewhere in it and the country peripherally peeks in through the major waterways. My character has a hard time maintaining a certain stance with the advent of television and all that; he becomes dis-illusioned and sort of topsy turvy. One minute he'll be talking about another minute and the next minute he'll be swearing by another which apparently is how he came by his name which is Charles.

When Charles was born his name was Evan. He went home to eat lunch which was across the street because the school is there. The tuna fish sandwich is being thrown out the kitchen window along with the string beans which begins the afternoon back in 1955.....Dave is amazed at how fast things get started.

It was a blue yellow day when the sky was black. Stephen is walking up the block towards the subway built in 1919. Back then people could get to work faster and get home. A woman will be breaking out of an F express and then Bill ambled back a few steps. There is also a unity or an uninfinity where two or more factions, including their roots, met and discarded old ties. O it will be a loose times in those days!

Which decadence and in what decade? Those ten questions were used frequently as model architecture when a reference is intellectually imperative and even then only when it was morally necessary. Alex pours a drink and looked sideways towards the boulevard. He will be a foreigner and he knows it all too well. Many people walk through those doors but none were sober in their approach.

Jasper plays Stars and Stripes Forever and cried into the crook of his arm and will be sorry. This writing begins here in the hemisphere which was encompassed and will be spacial.

AMBLE

Jack was not sure what his parents would name him or why. It was certain that he was not the great novel american. She excites six molecules with a brilliant discourse and disclosure. The two tracked flip side of sovereignty edges through her solar plexis. In fact the galaxy was filled with fists popping open with power and will close with an arthritic crackling like plastic. Up against a pole his shoulder looked over a newspaper at this guy. The sudden occurrence whereby they notice each other will cause a great commotion which acted like a bracket and gathers this contact into a specific and cautious moment. Brad was inescapable.

The armies of the north proceed south. The armies of the west proceeded east. The armies of the south will proceed north. The armies of the east may proceed west with the might of condition in their guns. The room number is in the central wing at the same time that Peter's address became exhilarated and flies out of the mailbox and was unaddressed by the mob. They kicked in place until the battlefield will bleed through the tension and this birth took to the external with pompous glory sparring in the street.

Who is the star? Lastly Arlene will come into their lives which have come into their own in the last split seconds. It is raining. It was snowing. The entire staff danced the Apocolypto and is mopping up the expulsion that isn't being mopped up. When he turned to the white uniform his brains took on a singular look. He executes the fusion with the speed of bone. On the corners of degeneration he spread his arms at length. It is gone before it will be gone. They were closely watched in the disturbance. Some clown raised his hand and asks what his name might be and in school they cut Clark's arms off. With permission from her parents, he returned and listened.

The day came when he is thinking of reconciliation. It is a plus lustre cycle that made his neck sweat. Nancy felt for him no matter what in the dark generation gap for his jittery presence denied. When they talked these funny little green things fall out of their mouth and into a tablecloth unseen. Perhaps the monitor would be more explicit than the replay and is not mocking the act of memory. As they strode into each other, Clifford makes a motion and April seconds it.

The germinal coagulant is this thing like not being happy which cropped up. The trapped can't flail evenly but Rocky took a degree and it was sunny if he graduated. It is not being stuck it was the stuck being. It was fucking with not is with fucking and that will not be denied at least not by this crowd who stood here.

Rod had something to say which makes it short. Janis didn't have the time to listen which causes confusion. Using like or as like like a poetic or as a lover seeks the definition of affinity of relationship that wasn't able in this day of age. Steve knew he has to get back to kicking if he was to keep this thing alive. The preamble states that "this writing begins here in the hemisphere which was encompassed and will be spacial" and will be spacial.

It excites me to hear good things about myself Pamela will think to himself eventually making it true.

INTERLUDICROUS

Dear Lover Person,

I hope you don't mind but there is no space left so I will write here for you. You know I am in the middle of something like writing but it has no title yet it is about names and about tense and about face and about conception simultaneously derived with the act of. It is dedicated to you, Gertrude, Marcel, Herman, and distantly

William and Johann Heinrich. I find you all interesting and worth living for and for you, with. There was something on my mind that is imperative. I find loving you related to breathing and music. Please accept my apocolyptia as a reason for any disturbance and love me back for it and other things. This is yours and this has been previously uncollected.

Signed.

But enough is not heard in the present of being for Claude and Francine who devised a plan to be looked elsewhere uncommonly for a taste sensational. Paul played summer soft ball in the five foot league under the tutelage which of course disappeared soon after he will grow upward. Sarah looks back as she left and might grab the door knob.

The trees hung loosely outside the glass keyhole that can sparkle with messages from the deep next door. This time the crowds were seated on their feet swinging an exclamation overhead which was doubted by the walls and is abhorred by the devout. Alan stood inbetween and is taken aback, awkwardly. He wanted the freedom to move out of place while Barbara stops kicking or mysteriously has access to something external which will scare them. He marvelously ducks.

The room was bare of essentials but will have a vertical pole that blocked one simple line of vision where things disappear. One track to be rejected which completely understated the entire composition as it were. What will make Robert qualify to achieve? What made her try to enter out?

They pumped closely together but will be in bed like a loft before they knew it. The school was across the street from Glenn when it is public and Timmy will eat anything even his lunch. That is his childhood which was nearby.

Tonight I heard a country change a man, Bruce said. Fortunately for her, said Sam.

The primary intercourse cleansing a silence that will be tense. With no previous significations they both looked into the void, dumbfounded. Donna combed her hair when she reappears absent mindedly closely beside the bed, naked. Her maker peeked out from her breast and waves hello to the whispering crowd. Perry folded over the pillow when he smiles. Let's make noise the grunts signified and defines.

There in the surface to surface transportation Axelrod enters the room. The external dream of driving a bus accidentally means something in this context and was. The eclipse made the day pale sunny in the moonlight.

Meanwhile Percy bought up all the blue property and charges phenominal compensation in a minimal way.

This was next on my addenda and how it comes about. It was not a good sign that blood appears in the exits and will be checked immediately by the chief. Something drastic was being. The skin fell by his wasteside so that it was up to him. In January the wind fell down from a rooftop clearly expressing the first moment of specific time. Arnold picks up the rake and picked it up together. Deborah moves slightly ever so while the television will be on, blaring.

Perhaps we could be talking about this moment, oh too late! This intervention didn't break it because it will be it in the eventuality that was now. Cary moved cautiously to the pole and faces the door. This was the drama that is happening. Denise will reach back and faced him squarely while Christopher stares out into the obstructed view.

Christmas came by in the season as it will snow in 1958 almost moving. Lenny was Wally's childhood spy who writes in his secrets behind a dark shadow. Children will be kids who are spacious and were indiscriminate. The stalemate grew fresh.

This may or may not be part of it.
What to do about nothing.
Schizophrenic communicado lurking in everyone.
Borrowing from some immediate epiphany.
The added factor of additional information.
The added factor of addition in formation.
The formulation of accumulation.
It is steel in the winterized snowdrops.

This may or may not be part of it.
The thought of character but not its development.
A turn of events and of phrases.
The nocturne of spaces sliding out of periphery.
The drive to the limits of personality ends in silence.

This may or may not be part of it.
The exact everyday thing is out of context.
In its place is the place it is in certainly.
A character is a thing in relation to its self.
One day language was not the thing expressed or local.
Confined to the cells we are born into with.
The bars on the windows are really there gridding.

He had a half hour left to say what he didn't say ever.

"I need you with warm calculation closing in around me like a bear hug administered overtly behind my back. They don't scold me for re-evaluating but I lived like that is to say I live like that underneath all my presence there was a reversion technique much like history. To love is to go out from that history into a larger confinement suitable for a future. Colors may clash but in my eyes this was not unsatisfactory because they are all here and on top of each other no matter how far their matter is scattered. Bring me the dice and I shall overturn the universe. But please, you must stay close because that is the way things are. Thank you for sharing your god given space with this midget."

She lifted her head like a curve ball and opens up so to speak.

"I am another person not just a woman or another person so that you are luscious in standing up to me as a figure. Don't forget your penis is a prime intrusion which draws us closer to withdrawal and a small explosion. I am torn. The liberation that snows outside that window appealed to my better sense of fusion by ice and generalization which is full of very but largely exposing acceptance. My escape in is through you and yours but I am certain of my importance because now I am rising up in a boner of self recognition. This expansion wants to hold your shrinkage and love you until do us part. We will get together next time around the cycle."

In the corner of this room which is tightly decorated there is lonliness which was a cramp in her stomach. Quincy quickly pulled himself apart searching for himself in relation to the hanging walls illusioned with story lines from beginning to end. Will they fall for the fat man's introduction?

In the corner of this room was a structure and is still there. Clancy sees that it has an underneath that will cling and was clinging to the underneath periphery. It was comfortable.

In the corner of this room will be a dream of inches begun in the core of molecules with uninhibited clocks branching out into microscopic yardsticks.

In the corner of this room is a fat image gesturing with a controlling factor hung between his abeyanced arms. Fred sees it as an obstruction and despised it for its complete and utterance. Penny frankly. She decides that the shape is worse than its bite which direction it takes and where it is gone. Barry spied on his friends and does so. Ralph kissed Virginia when it is a fourth grade Halloween.

In the corner of this room there could be a door swinging both ways in the wind outside and the tilt internally toward the hinge. It also does not exist. The outside did by the way and is really possible if the dueling pressures did not make the accessibility a pipsqueak and disappear almost entirely and entirely.

In the corner of this room there are two cells without names closed into copulation and captured in the open air by its own disposition. They can just imagine what it was like out there.

In the corner of this room there were centuries of corners once and still alive. They account for the mixup but also in crystal.

After *the* and the act of *the* they rested. The conversation meandered through the frost on the windows out onto the realm crystal superimposed on the horizon. What creature can fuck and coerce a simultaneous conception during a biological construction? Chuck stands on the same corner and smoked slightly along. The car crashes descend and such as intersections attempt the act of intra right up our alley. Delores handles them well and felt cocky.

A question presupposes and then demanded that Shelly remove herself quickly from the room. Craig looked at his watch and sees his lungs. Carlos will rub his dick in his sheets and excruciate. Yet the party is over and went well as long as it will be remembered. Nobody can leave the room and nobody does because they can't but it could and that accounts for the kicking in place, in place of moaning, that pretension of meaning and it was good and done.

The next day Howard awoke and tries to recapture what he most admired. She looks out onto the sky and declared it bright and beautiful even though her scar tissue is being used as clouds by the day broker. By comparison the relationship was drifting. Thomas seeks the elementary comfort of closed dark places and wanted a machine for a wife. They succeeded in gathering up while Elaine makes sounds denoting what will be percussive in the future and Keith is silent to the hilt.

It is amazing that they will not look back yet though....even the specific image was uneven in its appearance what with that kooky hat that will tilt to one side when someone noticed just hanging in this space like a nuisance. What the future held in store for me is appearing as vertical static on my television starring and co-starring in different shows.

Where is the blue executive in charge of decisions?

The voices of the future will be plastic but this character development was succinct as if the trees are quickly painted. Stuart was a shy boy who is shy. There are many people in many places who were elsewhere when they lived up to themselves. He was elegant when he is locked in, kicking. Things are getting better when they got worse in human reversion. Here was a bit of him.

As things turned out Susan appeared occasionally to help him which meant a light beam flows behind them always. She like man who like her. They like all admire the air jets that wrapped these things that they will be in light steel cages with motion slots. The grid of energies can turn to color after it rained with confinement and corners will be conquered in the middle. They are these things.

The day was indoors acting like the human condition that can't live together by being day and night and captivating when it made ends meet concisely.

There is no apprehension of the Fat Thing's corner and that decisions are discovered near its width. At least two conclusions for each conception zoom across the room and zig zagged like an outline like a shadow. These nearly indestructible bars of light invinced the steep valleys of history with future shock. Hillary has a mother which she still has inside her. The widened horizon is a pastry for a hungry diabetic and was a delicious devastation.

Communication is between the language where it takes clever dips into fantasy and meaning rode the dust beaming in. If they leave and go out no harm will come to them only they couldn't based on the concept of birth and the real mystery they forgot. Soon they will have to talk just to break the sound barrier into noise which was expression of a function. Kicking is a nice sound that will do.

Herbert narrows it down to negative space which remained at the center of peripheries as things slid passed. Clara screamed for comfort when he pushes in. It was the door made from windows they will find at the farthest point back in. The music is blasting up the pole which makes their inaudible speech a quite natural silence. There is so much explosion accumulated that all noise is vacuumed space and sounds that made it were fantastic. The meek existence of syntax and sequence and growth and development are unnoticed considerably in the loud scheme. The Intruder will be heard!

Up the pole through the depths of knowledge sunken back into a night of clouds rises this television shooting images at a cellular coagulation huddled in the corner. It was another day and Ted felt healthy and withdrawn. Margot still saw visions of greater things which the pole obscures. They will find that language will help but must intrude and describe a much lesser thing than expectations.

This was two days later. They had slept for two sections and it is a silver backdrop. The distorted aluminum reflection gives a true image of the situation as it stood before the wooden audience. The recognition and originally the cognition were blurred as is the distaste. The scope of fiction and its impressive formulations are real things to contend with. Impressed in the sense that the seamen were impressed into naval operations causing wars and independence which caused the kicking cement of cities to exist heavily. Deconstruction is the only way back forward. Behold beyond! Beyond being upheld by aluminum bricks might lie truth as it might have existed later. One thing is known for sure.

Personally we thought it is time to change that one thing that is a massive construct between two rivers. Even the invention of cancer points to this but ascension leaves behind the stayed. Of course these bodies are the loose ends of that form. The options are to drag it along or cut looser and tie into what the environment proves humorously. Give me liberty *and* give me death!

When words swallow their own meanings things made more than sense. Jeremy wanted to shut up while the world explodes. There is comfort in small territory and great explorations involved. Ginny pierced her ears and grew over it but pimples are a major crisis. Complexions are unimportant in the mirror in fact in the mirror all things have a way of being the same value and didn't really matter or carry any space to speak of.

She was inherently human and disagrees with this which changed the complexion of the entire unstable. A pair of wings flutter up the pole and changed the channel. For now Joshua and Louisa felt the floor entirely rise to the occasion along with all the space in the universe

19, 70, 4

JANUARY
12345678910111213141516171819202122232425262728293031
the structure of an accident is full of purpose
FEBRUARY
12345678910111213141516171819202122232425262728
like a religion with more wishes than not
MARCH
12345678910111213141516171819202122232425262728293031
and the king of jews swallows two mountains
APRIL
123456789101112131415161718192021222324252627282930
and again and again
MAY
12345678910111213141516171819202122232425262728293031
the mistake is twice the person I am
JUNE
123456789101112131415161718192021222324252627282930
maintenance near the broken leap can settle it once
JULY
12345678910111213141516171819202122232425262728293031
the other once
AUGUST
12345678910111213141516171819202122232425262728293031
becoming grown up in the ruins and puddles
SEPTEMBER
123456789101112131415161718192021222324252627282930
reflections in a crack, brilliant rivers
OCTOBER
12345678910111213141516171819202122232425262728293031
sparse one two, sparse, one two, buckle
NOVEMBER
123456789101112131415161718192021222324252627282930
I can touch the roof of floor in unison
DECEMBER
12345678910111213141516171819202122232425262728293031
forever in your debt

"The white has lost its tail
the gentle has grown hard
and won't leave its place
and between the slow and the gray
the commas weep periods."

Jean Hans Arp

Herm Freeman

THREE ROOMS ON E. 9th STREET

One Room/Spring 1975
New York City

3 ROOMS ON E. 9th STREET - Spring 1975-Spring 1976

E. 9th Street began in Park Slope, Brooklyn where Ezra and I lived with an old friend, S.L. for about 2 months while I recovered, got my 'hack' license (a job) and found an apartment.

350 East 9th Street was a small, 3 room apartment which, in turn, gave rise to 3 distinct periods in my life. In one 'room,' I was alone for the very first time in my life and had to adjust to the separation from R and a way of life which had become habitual. The apartment was slowly transformed into my mirror image. I made paintings directly on the wall (mostly 'blood-red') and hung an intricate string matrix across my ceiling. The 'living' room was becoming a catacomb of my own 'neuroillogical' system of behavior.

I found strength and solace in the rebellious rejection of meaning which I was finding in my continuing explorations of Dadaism and Futurism. H and I began a subtle bending and folding of these delinquent attitudes in our music and art and to it we added our own rounded edge of middle class, 'sit-com' morality. We called our version NEONEO and DODO (the actual 'doing' of Neoneo).

I also needed some new (neo) character to act out my new (neo) life of 'positive rejection.' I wanted to convince myself that I was once again on the rise and so I named this new (neo) feeling PHIL DEMEYES ('dem eyes [demise] gonna rise again'). I was playing with being positive about being negative and 'vices verses.'

It was somewhere 'in this room' that H & I, with R.S. (saxophone), performed at St. Marks Church as NOYES in our first public musical performance. It was a synthesizer and tape extravaganza playing such hits as MOCEAN SHRIEK, GUITAR MASSAGE (playing electric guitar with objects) and a saxophone, 'paddle-ball' duet.

But the pressure of 'acting as if' and the vast loneliness of floatation nearly shook me to pieces. I needed to escape the center of my chaos. I needed a *neo* perspective to match my *neo* character. To be 'reborn' I opted to go back in time and join the young Dadaists and Gertrude Stein and turn the century with my new friends and comrades. So I packed up my pieces and flew to Paris to live the fantasy and spread the word of NEONEO. I was entering another 'room,' room to grow.

Paris did everything I had expected and more. I met three extraordinary women (new women/*neo* women). One was an American painter on her way to a Greek Island to study who changed her plans so that she could spend the first week with me in Paris. We sat in cafes in Montparnasse and talked of NEONEO. On one of our gallery expeditions (a Max Ernst Show) I got caught by the attention of another woman who 'coincidentally' crossed my path at Le Drugstore the next day and left me her number. When I was once again alone in Paris, I called her. In that second week in Paris I communicated with A.R., we met for a drink and we began our love affair with the 'idea' of a love affair with each other. For the 'time being' it was perfect.

During this brief period I had also been given an apartment to live in by an old friend whom I had contacted when I had first arrived in Paris. Then, at the same time that A.R. and I were beginning our adventure, I met another woman with yet another kind of relationship to me. She was married and had grown children and was on a 'holiday' alone. We fell in love immediately and played out this 'immoral and illicit' fantasy with great style and lots of Art. When she left to return to England I moved in with A.R. and got to see and hear Paris from the inside. She listened and shared my neo feelings and life began to flow through me once again.

After two months of love and ex-patriotism, I was complete enough to want to return 'home.' When I finally did return (to the 'third room') in September of 1975, I was a *neo* man. I was immediately greeted with a challenge to my new life. The BRAINARD/FREEMAN NOTEBOOKS (Gegenschein 1112), which I had sent to the printer before I left for Paris and had expected to be completed and awaiting my arrival, had been returned with a note from the printer refusing to print the 'pornographic sketches' of Joe Brainard and Herm Freeman. After my initial disappointment and indignation at this outrageous censorship, I actually became pleased that something I was doing had been rejected by a 'proper morality.' It became like a battle scar and an inspiration towards a more active pursuit of the dismemberment of ridiculous, outdated values.

It was also at this time that I began running a poetry reading series with Ed Kulkosky at the then, unknown CBGB's where the then, unknown bands like TELEVISION, PATTI SMITH, THE SHIRTS and TALKING HEADS were just beginning to play. In conjunction with the series we published a newsletter which is where my NEONEO MANIFESTO first appeared. I also gave a reading and performed some 'minimal tone poems' (as Phil Demise, the *phenomenalminimalist*) which was my first NYC poetry performance since 1970 (PHRAGMENTS & PHRASES with dancer Larry Clark).

T was in the audience that night and we were introduced after the reading. I went home with T instead of going back to R's (still on MacDougal St.). R and I had recently begun seeing each other again on a very tentative basis. That evening with T was my first true moment of 'life without R' since 1968.

My new life also included the beginnings of new friendships. I finally met Guy Beining, in person, a poet whom I had corresponded with and published in Gegenschein. We began our BICENTENNIAL PIECE OF MIND, my first collaboration. I also met, through R, Jeffrey Lohn, an early Soho conceptual artist/musician and unlicensed plumber and, after having convinced my father to advance me $5000 to take a raw space and make something out of nothing (a gallery and performance space), Jeffrey and I went out looking. As I was looking into the future, GEGENSCHEIN 1314 (NEONEO DODO EX-GQ 1314) appeared (the concept was based loosely on Richard Kostelanetz/Henry Korn/Mike Metz' ASSEMBLING) and tried to further the NEONEO cause.

The writings of this period were an overlapping of my experimentations. They continued to list the disparate abstractions that flew wildly around very human emotions. They remained as flights through the 'clouds of issues,' hiding the intensities in the aftermath of floatation. Slowly the 'ideas' of my own retrospection became the issues, and anarchy in its purest Kropotkin-sense became the hovering cloud that touched each new occurrence. I once again acknowledged and celebrated my own ignorance and stupidity, taking away their power. I continued to explore the 'other side of zero,' the negative, the 'ex' side, what I didn't know, and I tried to do it without preconceptions and the usual judgments. I was still trying to somehow link together the opposing qualities of my own personality and give it a name ('anarchistic zen dada'). At the same time I was on a positive expedition in search of the new feminine part of my relationship to ideas and love. All in all it was a powerful uprising and it began to take me up with it.

T had agreed to move in with me and when we finally found the 'dream' at 293 7th Avenue I named it THE GEGENSCHEIN VAUDEVILLE PLACENTER, a womb of disparate performance. It was the beginning period, again

the subventures of Ääbez & Grandö translated by LZÄ

Ääbez! What are you doing?

I was predicting what you would do. And I was right!

Why is it that I always find nothing
Ah, there's One

I've always been more down to earth than you, Grandö!
I'll show him..

Let's see if Ääbez can predict this

I predict that you're standing behind me, looking very proud, head cocked to one.

Phil Demise

WHAT I DON'T KNOW FOR SURE

-1
what is it like to be out
in the deep space between
two or more

without

and how come

-2
simply because

-3
a blanket
answer bending
and through the complete

always

-4
son of a

-5
there
by the way
what is it like
to be like

-6
laugh and the whole world

-7
events turn of and dizzy
connective tease

the flicker oh suffering

-8
not knowing the unknown
knowing what

-9
a blue gold

-01
and the proper noun for me
of distance
behind which I

-02
the situation

-03
the taste of the good life
is air but of

course not
clear

-04
it's all the same
to him
unlike me

-05
what is going
(on,off,in)

-06
how to

-07
all my fears are of things
I know nothing about

-08
regrettably but
nonetheless

-09
the dull dilemma
the cerebellum

-001
the terror of practice
makes
perfect screech

-002
working for a living
writing for a death

the successive failures
the linear

-003
what end

-004
the last tree
to occupy

the first tree

-005
gulp

-006
putty murmur
I write, I wrote

-007
that nothing
and each

-008
I've had accumulation
up to here
and there
since the copper voice
and the technology
of symptoms

-009
perhaps what I do know

-0001
the direction of movement
but just

-0002
similarly the same occurs
but the circumstance
goes round and round

-0003
it's getting there

-0004
that counts as well
as this
is

LOVE YOU TO BITS

the crescent lash
the whipping arc of mystery

*

my voice never changed

*

you in particular

*

clickety-clack
the muscle clock

*

no trump

*

shiny blue infrequency
masked exposure

*

plenty

*

*

one another

*

the double pink line

*

warm crush
scarce waste

*

shrugs

*

ample, example

*

blubbering
the talk of the town

*

(them)

*

conquering unhitched security

*

*

unconditionally
thrusting prepositions on numbness

*

the ruler without measure
decrees accidental distance

*

(cranky)

*

(before we knew it)

*

two bits

*

the teeth of no solution breaking
the skin, the bones, the heart,
the blood, the spine, the brain,
the spirit, the neck

*

eclipsed without blockage

*

the personification of suicide
expanding with sucking regularity

*

*

far at hand and holding

*

all systems gone

*

the old lady living outside her shoe

SSTRANGED

*

singular

*

sparse partner
envelop

lopped off

*

the neck
the connection

conk!

*

cash shackles

*

et
ext
inf

*

name one

*

this too too two
solid flash

*

*

perhaps, possibly, maybe,
MIGHT

*

on one
condition
in
condition

*

back to this
back to back

*

pop the question!

*

will you marr
y me

*

proof of

*

the matter
them at her

*

legalized absorption

*

*

sucked out by uncertainty
maternal cobras
click

*

kick cock

*

meaning is a definitive disease
meaningless is an infinite antibody

mind is only in your head

*

everything is relative
by comparison

*

I like you
I, like you

*

pairation

*

re
pair
airation
seepage

*

*

running toward from

*

commune schism
b*aa*roke

*

it's over 'cause we stopped

TINY STORY

This is a story about self effusement..............I am the perpetrator......He stares at his wrist until a clock appears... He sees there isn't much time left....the little hand is on the big hand.....He jumps out the window and lands in a luncheonette...They are waiting for service......What is she....

As he gets up to water the plants he forgets.....Their hands are there...They are in places....The strings that hang from the top floor have fists tied to the bottom....He moves toward the telephone and smashes his head against white knuckles....He falls (preconscious) to the ceiling below.....

She is undressed....I am the perpetrator....He takes off her skin and bites off the ends of her bones...Pieces of death drip from the light fixtures...Lies scoot around like mice...They laugh at the silliest things....What a switch....He comes to to die again......Human splinters are coming out of his ears......

When he awakes he is sleeping......

EXISM

We are all exed out when we enter crossed. We are all crossed. We are all disallowed. We are all below and beyond the time we existed. We are all dehumanized by length. We all expect towards expiration. We are all sectional and disavowed. We are all decomposing excellently. We are all living on exblocks with exwives. We are all convinced that because it is the way it is it is going forward. We are all exiting the future into history.

THE WILD BLUE

the Xist Doctrine the blunder the pound the crown
victory of velocity over the punk progression of
random numbers the exsequential takeoff down the
primrose gully out of the body into the arms of

space

the counter clockwork time piece the spill the
broken guppy the excruciating reaction to the
historical future backing up

THE FIFTEEN' BETWEEN NOW AND CATCHING A BUS

we are all situated exquisitely without appendages
inside the body we occupy whenever whatever but
however not forever whichever we exhale first and
and and and this exevolves back into advancement
and flaming conjunctions presuppose the exlink that
holds our act together with reactionary bondage and
fiery soliloquies that are rocket black extensions of
our trapped existence puffing up with amputations and
bits blown out of proportional mulling over exits
which are bus routes and exact change fingering the
entrance with masturbatory excitement

NONOS SERMON

no answer no no is the answer and left us nowhere no not
us huh the exralph exists no not because but did not not
explain that it was not quick enough no not quite so no
answer was not it but ex it ralph and down pops exralph

quietly decomposed

HOORAY FOR ME

it is falling apart like a permanent just sagging in
the wet horizon of a silly madness which explains all
reckless shifts yet to be taken (I can't decide which
way to explode) what form what texture what difference

the one problem is transition and the other is occupation
in terms of space and me in it full of every nuance I
can imagine helpless as a wind in fire to keep it going
full of spectrum hot as blazes and substantial meaning

the feeling is mutual the prehistoric tyrannical sex
power more powerful than a locomotive shoving leit motifs
through the tunnel with the speed of sound translating
the silence of which it is born into the silence for which

it dies

FREE DUMB

Here we are I mean here I am occasionally unsettling.
We I mean I.

Freedom's just another unjust word like separation.
Like like.

The children we don't have are suffering and we
I mean I can't conceive of it blowing off.

The edge of the wind is confused.

The two sides to every question beat each other up.
Answers bleed from bruises and smell like aggression.

The falling came in time to catch the ground.

Looking forward to not remembering the pain of memory.
Time zones are deceased.

May they I mean I rest in peace like wood.

LOOP D. LOOP

this life goes on through the loops pursuing further issues
running tons of fingers through the semi rounded sacks of
thrust with a complete finality each time it begins

look at any clock   time is circular   look at any
clock

our mouth is full of dreams   a network of invisibility
a bag of distance hangs from our forehead and rattles
with a seductive silence   giving the mind a concept
for the real thing and the space between touch and desire
to touch

burns

SONNET TO A SAXOPHONE BACKACHE

at last I can feel the pain
whoopee
horns of plenty horns
delicacies
deep drops screeching and they are brown
thin lines of thickness occupying thick dreams
body tremors reject the silence of introduction
bird spurts cut the sky into soft shreds
the sudden ascent comes back through holes in the scale
a galaxy of shoulders
shrug
and the light
disappears
in the light

JUNIOR FROLICS

the The of It breaks its hook
the hard chair rocking back and forth
seeks an orange brain made of dark wood
to speak highly of itself
in the presence of the past

the trumpet is called for

is it rain outside in the afternoon
tonight in 1957 now?

farmer gray kicks the mice
one by one they fly off the earth
each going north for the winter

this guy I am is stuck in the ice
a series of screws twist through the cushion
the seat of my pants stuck to its guns

in the sun a chip off the old block
turns shadows into sleep
picking up the pieces
of Uncle Fred's empire

MOCEAN

this is being
provided
by the sculpture in your atmosphere,
a sculpture made from wind
and the speed of velocity rushing
through a soft fruit
accelerating the branches
like the imaginary connections
between space and trees.

I make up
the relationship
because why
not why
not since
we share the planet
of expression
since the curves are not circles
and fulfill
the soft supposition of completion.

MORE ORPHAN THAN NOT

has my dada left mr. me for another sun?

it has left the entire earth flat.
circumlocution will never be the same
and neither will mr. me and his circle
of friends squaring off for a skirmish.
latching on to the indentation like a trench
lapsed into consciousness like the nipple
in the bud pressing in on the aroma.

mr. me never was and never will be
the same.

SNOW IS IN THE EYE OF THE FLOWER

it Is very precipitation like canvas politicians.
all Something long, I have been approaching.
chasing Like whiskey, this crackling, young crack.
this. this Snow wing. this. this Coming up, yeah.

water is a flower
electricity is a flower
radio is a flower
river is a flower
conversation is a flower
interview is a flower
art is a flower
flower is part flower

NECK AND NECK

the moon weighs 16,000 tons
after it has a taste of oxygen

my bottle has eaten the milk

the moon and the bottle
have two things in common
both of which are
the moon and the bottle

and lastly
the first objective
is to burst open
and give the guy air

in the meantime
the anger coagulates in the neck

many moons ago the phase shifted
into small bullets moving backwards

my milk was shot through the heart
my heart was shot through the head

the moon was full of it
breakneck speed crawled up its back

the cow jumped
and eclipsed my light head

in the space of one second
somewhere in the years to come

a bullet deadened my lunacy
the last straw drank the milk

and the moon jumped over the cow

TRAPPED

in, of rubble, middle of and of course this course
on which on course, off course, of course that trouble
and debris which is

here in the matter, in the matter of course, of what is,
of what is the matter, of course, off course, the middle
of which is

debris and trouble, in, of rubble and me of course

THE INVISIBLE TEAM OF MULES MAKE ASSES OF THEMSELVES

connective tissue should not be left on the kitchen sink
dissatisfaction is a relative distance carved into trees
boy o boy meets girl o girl alone in a basket of kilometers
touching parts are torn to numb shreds like gasping sea
    weed
cunts and cocks become ice cubes banging up against
    scotch
feelings round off to the nearest tenth and coagulate
circulation bungles its first route and cracks in half
the uncommon stock of simultaneity splits two for one
blood vessels sink into the blood and drown in bioillogical
    wasted time
going down hill becomes a figure in reach
every circle has two or more centers puffing up the pure
    form
rocks of air buffer the space with blasphemic cushions

the end

Nobody knits like Wendy knits.
WendyKnits
719 S. Los Angeles St.
Los Angeles, CA 90014
Wholesale inquiries only
WHERE ARE WE, A-BOEZ?
THIS, GRANDÖ, IS THE MUSEUM OF CONTEMPORARY TRADITION.
YOU MEAN...
NO, WE ARE JUST VISITING!
PHEW, I THOUGHT...
NO WAY, GRANDÖ, WE'RE TOO INSIGNIFICANT !!
POOR GRANDÖ
MAYBE YOU ARE, A-BOEZ, BUT NOT ME!

Phil Demise

And so Americans go to Paris and they are free not to be connected with anything happening. That is what foreignness is, that it is there but it does not happen.

Gertrude Stein

Phil Demise

ONE ROOM TOO
Summer 1975
Paris

AN AMERICAN IN PARIS BY GEORGE

*

I am flying between two points
and I am the shortest distance

*

especially when the clouds are underfoot

*

out the plane window
the other side of glass

*

add "so far" to any statement

*

we made connections
Paris is not flat
it is the same but somewhere else
somewhere else it is the same
but it is not here now
now somewhere else it is not here
we are still somewhere else
and here
it is like that all over
(so far)

*

accidentally it happened
it just so happened
it happened

*

wherever it went
so went whoever

*

well he accepts that and accepts that
and that and that and that
and takes that and takes that and take that
and that and that and that and he accepts that
except for one thing
that thing
except for that one thing

*

I don't doubt it

*

will return broke not broken
the neoneography of Paris is a thin range
filled with rain and still winds
Paris needs saxophones and fire hydrants

*

women here speak same language with more pronunciation
I speak same language with more punctuation
when I speak they listen and noone understands
just like in America
the world is very similar to the world

*

there are only three spaces between four numbers

NEONEO ANARCHISTIC verite POLITICLEMIC

!1

parts of bodies in special disorder march behind
the pinkies in ribonucleic fashion

brains, thumbs, livers, arches, ribs, lungs, eyeballs,
knuckles, wrists, blood clots, lips, ear lobes and

disconjunctive etceteras and and and and etcetera

the disarray of pink colors, the black periods....
a galactic overview of historic sleepwalks,,,,
a coma removed from the body

what's left, what's new

a revolution, a counter clock, *la perfection meme*
unemployed from function marching through the
identical struggle, the indentity

in the month between december and january
the parade descends up the celebration: "RISET"
(pinkies scream at the bottom of lungs)

low decibels shake the crust of the earth
it has begun in the microcosmic pistols of the intellect
in the asystemic strands of explosive pink flesh
walking off the hands like bullets

the shock felt squarely round
QUIRKS IGNITE!

!2

where, for Art, the

hovering helicopter, the in
sect capability, the montaging vision

conducting the electrical voices of infinity
into a dome of pink noise

pieces de resistance

what is left is right
the apex of direction
the culmination of fragments
the distant Echo of all echoes

white into red
unity of unions

the cooperative individual embattled
with the coopted singularity of systematized groups,
with the horizontal politic of party lines
which the ocean imagines as horizon

neoneo anarchy is a timeless bomb
ticking in the body politic

we are all employed by Existence
workers are the living proof

the BIG PRODUCTION is a factory of air

!3

l'offre et la demande

1. disarm, rip from limb to limb,
tear off the shoulders we lean on

2. suck your pinky and absorb its small connection
to the certainty of the grasp

3. hold a little in the palm of your finger
a little at a time where there is no time

4. offer that small *verite* to the pink pool
of blood and white sweat

5. let the Singular Extension coagulate
the shreds of our dismemberment

6. join the Parade of Parts

7. deny the Facade of Partitions

8. let all the sounds of separation RISET into space
as One Signal announcing the NEONEO *verite* that we
exist as a community of questions

9. that we are greater than we THINK

10. that we are what's left and we are pink

OUI WE

raulin descending a nude staircase her left hand
watching a perfect sanction increase in size o
pen jotting slight shifts of birds' names enclosed
severely in my open eyes opening with (width) open
arms the expanse of culture and the glass steel arches
triumphantly diving across the ocean invisibly connecting
the concrete abstraction of cities visible in the eyes
of skin which the brain sheds like a snake and paints
the stares the color of air and our bodies the color
of evaporated blood as we (oui we) like

ICI REPOSE VERITE

ice poses as heat this january in september
very actually an opaque cellophane and light
passing through disproven blips dotting the
eyes of bantam cocks batting the flashes of
the mockrocosmos lying flat on inclinations
actually mistaken as ironic mutations of an
air about them in the morning of evening out
rounding off puffing up and excruciating

like holding water in your hand

The Key to Making Art Phil Demise

DETOUR DE FARCE

the special requirements of completions
the air space grounded in the gravity of situations
the opening of new circles
"the big scissors to cut your toenails"
the drifting tomatoes nailed to the atmosphere
the danceless structure of amputation
the inconstant flower

an anarchical circulation blocked by doors
an oversized insufficient ego
an ocean without water
an anthill made of footprints

on the level
on the upheaval of descension
on the positive negation

and the shredded tendrils
and the snazzy borders holding back
and the expanse of dreams in a box

an and on the
conjunction

q = a

the foreign occurrence of politic qnd correspondence
the next phqse in q broken leg
the musculqture of qmendments
the qll reqdy existence
the how ever in the present tense

pour exqmple:
qesthetic goo spells flqt mountqins
with the verticql horizon spinning down
through eye-cons of vision
the opposite holds true like qn upstqrt
qnd so the blqckbird is q fuzzed spectrum
q corporqtion of every movement
qnd sits in my pinky when I drink teq

flowers flowers flowers of flowers
qnd qn egg

FRAGMEANT

sunday god cover your soupish song with ice
obelisks of air gather these muscles
dead to the interior of my return
the closets aren't the reason and we know it
no closets are the reason and we know it
we rejoin the strength of chains
that we are iron and we are the closets

*

what is the language that we forget
and we mistake as light
our inertia is the fountain between the months of time
and the dry wind which a sick soul discolors
seeing the complementary crease in us
as the paper crumpled with the emblem of defeat
captured in another age with the gills
of prehistoric fish

RIDING SOUTH THROUGH THE SUN

a transmutation of Tristan Tzara

noise maintains the soft muscles in fruit
the intoxicating dance of secretions
the sweet tissue lingers there
covering the new slashes of brief moments

in the horizon remains a small blanket
of water running through vast tunnels
mashing the particularly small coefficient
of my love
the door dances with sudden electricity

transfixed by these eclipsed desires
blood accelerates and palpitates
the possibility of private agreements
the inconsistency of glistening water
on the bottom of the sun's body
by the miracle found between the mask
so clear so new
the movement of the eye the quick sound
of a moving bell
the sudden exposure
of the yellow rolling dance
tells why

the advantage you sang travels in a circle of vapor
an even flow of flames from the volcano you are
that leads to the grave
on the tight wings of arduous chance

and the shape
the world
a coffin of flowers
the world
a closed box for a flower

one flower flower for the bouquet of flowers flowers
a door of cigarettes made of flowers
a small locomotive powered by flowers
a pair of gloves for these flowers
in the skin of flowers
as these flowers flowers flowers of flowers
and an egg

JAMIE

exSeptional this month and secondly
fourwiths well come exist TENTS
in buckets Brussels sprouting down
rapport exactly almost raindrops

even though

GIVE ME A HAND

the cowering thickness of loneliness
makes mice grow in my words like buttons
they are meant like the sun's light is meant
for us
a result of involuntary equations
concentric attitudes surrounding the fingers
they just chopped off
the disallowed appendage searching for something
to hold onto

The door to the invisible must be visible.

Rene Daumal

Herm Freeman

ROOM TO MOVE
Fall/Winter 1975
New York City

CONCEPTIONS VAUDEVILLE

1. Duet for a Pregnant Woman: a dance. A pregnant woman does a solo.

2. Group Conversation Piece: A large group gathers on stage as if waiting in the lobby during the intermission of this piece and they begin talking about what they thought of the piece. After 15 minutes there will be an intermission and the play begins in the lobby with the audience discussing the piece they just witnessed. The actors watch.

3. You design a poster for an art exhibition stating on the poster that the poster is the exhibition.

4. You invite 100 people to a 12x15 room for a Bring Your Own Space Party.

5. The Just Marred Car Train Horn Improvisation: Ten dissimilar cars gather at Ten A.M. Sunday morning at 7th avenue and 28th St. each car decorated with a hand painted sign on their trunks JUST MARRED. They travel downtown honking their horns with an ear for music. The train stops at Sheridan Square and the signs are removed and thrown in the trash cans and the cars go off in different directions.

6. Make a list of Conceptions and put them in book form for others to realize.

7. Advertise a concert for the Malharmonic Symphony Orchestra to be held in a large space suitable for a large audience. At 8:30 P.M. the curtain rises on a small orchestra of well dressed musicians. The program notes will read: THE MALHARMONIC SYMPHONY ORCHESTRA PRESENTS: A JOKE. The conductor walks formally into position, raises his baton and the orchestra plays a dramatic 'A' tone. A

member of the audience then jumps up and screams J O K and the orchestra plays a soft 'E' tone. Curtain.

8. Boredom Piece: Have curtain rise on a stage set up like an audience with rows of chairs. Actors enter and are seated as an audience would be seated and talk and mill around naturally. The lights on stage blink on and off indicating the play will start. The lights on stage are then turned off and the house lights go on. The play continues until the last member of the audience leaves.

MY SUMMER VACATION

by Philip Demise

This summer I had a very good and bad time. In the bad time I spent it just doing nothing in the city and sitting and thinking. In the good time in the city I spent it just sitting and doing nothing special except feeling good about myself and the situation I am in somehow. Then later on we went to the country to be with nature and all her goofy tricks. It was great doing nothing and having all the sounds around you say "Good for you." But nature though good and beautiful and all that doesn't know really how to play with me since I make up the rules for the games I love most and it is dumb and doesn't understand. But it is fun anyhow because it makes me feel good somehow. Anyway, I made friends with this little fish in the topical tank who understood and talked to me in bubbles like a cartoon. He kept saying things even though I really couldn't hear him say nothing. Soon we will be going back to the city and then school starts again.

NUTSHELL

To celebrate the denunciation, to celebrate its steadfast adherence to the slick walls and open windows, would be the proper leap from the doldrums. The excommunication of products of which I am the factory and the simple process of one by one reinstitution of selected things. Brand new definition based on impression, the flower of definition. The knowledge of nothingness does not dissolve the body and that is the physical dilemma in a nutshell.

THE SKY CHILDREN

the cloud muscles ripped
the sky children racked their brains
the eyes are balloons
the overview danced on the head of a pin
the sky is inflated cellophane
the body is coagulated oxygen

they can never land
they spend saturday on sunday
they actually are not
they entice spasms
they are the circle above the line

the accidents are acceptable
the government is air
the community is translucent silver
the currency is necessity
the exchange rate is speed

they work when they have free time
they marry for moments at a time
they discontinue time for a time
they have no time for time
they die on time
they naturally want peace

the belly aches are soft
the homicide dwindles
the language is wings
the sky children flock alone
the absolute is broken into sections
the absolute is never reached
the absolution is absent directly

they adhere to here
they are cohesive fission
they are scattered clumps
they are a multiplicity of additions

the sky children have air rocks for muscles
the sky children become the water for their own thirst
the sky children hover forever
the sky children never look up
the sky children occupy their own spaces
the sky children have no shadows

they are invisible entities
they necessitate unique structures

the panic excruciates and fades out
the initial eclipse slivers through the urge
the sky children break the glass
and fall to earth as angels

they say "come into the chaos and that's an order!"
they scream "come into the chaos and that's an order!"
they penetrate our results with:
COME INTO THE CHAOS AND THAT'S AN ORDER!

the sky children are namely being an anonymous society
which is synonymous to namely being mental
    not governmental

the sky children bounce off the earth's structure

EXERCISING

lifting the muscles in the gate
opening the lightning bolt
sitting on the tip
of the last dendrite
flexing a small fist
through the absence of water
flowing through the streams of synapse

wading for the pearl
of continuous stoppage
and the leap across

a herd of sleeping pulsations
bang up against the soft nothingness

nothing awakens, nothing sleeps
just a deep unheard of rumbling

THE ULTERIOR BEING

the beginning ends with the beginning
bending through the calculus of clouds
leaving giant traces of commingling
jumping off the edge into another edge

ing words indicate the on going on and on

as with the tree's ego bolted to the earth
the beingness of things bolted to the word
to the particle of physics blinking in the fog
the second before the first holds our presence

the ulterior being being the human of being
projecting the ends with calculating obesity
expecting rewards for excellence and living
a second after existence
as if that's not far enough removed
it gets tense with future

and ing begins to end to be
the being being

META ONA SUNDAY

1. the metamorphosis of *Because*
can be traced to a lack
of sufficient predication
and *Becomes*

the untouchable floating tonic
disconnected abstraction
flashing across the split
second transitions
and the raucous screams
of excitement and terror
and the dismembrance of history
and the frenzied surgical performance
and the Constant of disbelief

there is no direction in space
it is just going from the point you are

returning is an attitude not a direction

the neoneo quick return to essence
one first before the second
an unrecognizable style
full of the life force
for no reason

2. a list of connecting circles (like a SPRING)
fresh water, new season, thrust of metallic
the area is clumsy and inconstantly spinning
with inarticulate desires for resolution
but it leaves and enters a new sphere
unsatisfied and constantly tempted by fulfillment

things push against it from both sides
causing the illusion of accessibility

new forms are really old forms never realized

the multicycle is ridden behind the illusion
of steering mechanisms

(accidents will happen)

3. exactly full of nothing spectacular
this actor goes home to die of sleep
without the least bit of satisfaction

the sleep narration is mute
sounds of velocity rush past the window
the ocean
the desperation of tonal procedure
the unharnessed tonic of being
atonal and less than subdominant, *alive*

Herm Freeman

NEO DREAMS

drops of incessant hesitation
condense on the rainbow
in my glass eye

I see them when I re-
treat
into the dense color

I taste them in a mouth
that is in my mouth

and the words that sleep
in their moisture

somewhere along my own lines
have been dissolved

in the new dream
the neo dream
I am wrapped in a blanket
of bark
the price on my head
sticks out like a crown
of dark mathematics
and the addendum

in the opening

NEONEO MANIFESTO

UNIVERSION

The portent of communication and the pretension of loaded words blast you in the face of all the definitive opinions that exercise their autonomical functions as systems.

There is nothing like perpendicular verticals. There is nothing like a metaphysic for constipation. There is nothing like metaphorical similes. There is nothing like them. They are terrific. They are unbelievable. They are fantastic.

There is understanding the elements of a situation. There is an elemental understanding of polarity and the equality of power and attraction.

The story of a life is one story.

IT IS AN ATTITUDE AND THAT'S NOT AN ORDER!

Neoneo rejects the boundaries that create value and embraces the free escape of elements and the worth of the atmosphere they create. It expects nothing and gets something in return. It surrounds. Neoneo is the end of art as a separate and mystical existence. Neoneo is nothing special, just spacial.

Objects are created to fit into a neoneo atmosphere. The creation does not embody the concept, it acts as its momentary focal point and a shadow of the attitude out of which a strange but ordinary light burns out the necessity for judgment. Neoneo is an imperfect aura that hovers above the governments of enclosure and signifies nothing in particular.

Neoneo is your own attitude plus the process of understanding its everchanging elements. Depression, impedance, speed, autodestruction, sloppiness, impotence, carelessness, fertility, accidentals, fallibility, procreation, infallibility, systemathematicality, antidisestablishment-neoneoisticalness, etcetera, all of equal worth in relation to the process of understanding and its embodiment in things.

It is the *in*tention of process not the *con*tention of realization. It is the knowledge that information is useless. It is an antistructure antimatter attitude towards the process through which realization may take shape. It is the acceptance of the WORTH of all things even if there is a rejection of a particular's company.

Noeoeo is the end of all movements yet it is the beginning of all movement into the free space of anarchical equality. All good things have a beginning. NEONEO!

DUOVERSION

Neoneo is the opposite.

THE NEONEO MORNING

the neoneo morning is an oblique salmon
flowing through the stiff arc of anticipation
it is firm in its non commitment
it is pink in its possibilities
it is over as it begins

momentarily continuous

NEON EGO

it is an attitude through which things as they are are strained without effort and then reappear (recreate) as a microscopic and monumental psychoillogical lounge chair on the deck of polyamnesia. it is memorable only for its comfort. it is aqualitative but holds the highest quality lack of opinions like extraterrestrial veins running through cosmic wrists. it is immediately understood by every body. the bones in the mind require liquid space therapy but always come around to your way of thinking in a neoneo eventuality. Every thing is atypical atonal asymmetrical alive and indefinitely around. it is a special fund raiser. it is based in feeling good but by no means is it stationed there. and feeling good does not even exist. it unevenly exists in neoneos of chemicals and electrons. all things enter the neoneoeye at the same value and leave the body after due circulation neoneoized with painful splendor and a white acceptance. if some thing happens it is neoneo and blessed with constant kisses. neoneo was born from between kinetic thighs but lives as a potential threat to all systems. neoneo is the asystem of the universe.

OPTIMUM OPTIMISM

everything is fine
I mean it
everything is terrific
really
things are okay
I'm not kidding
everything is great
no shit
things are excellent
I mean it

Each second is a universe, the second I live is the second I live in...

Italo Calvino

Herm Freeman

GEGENSCHEIN VAUDEVILLE PLACENTER 1976-1978 New York City

THE GEGENSCHEIN VAUDEVILLE PLACENTER - 1976-1978

The Placenter was officially born on April 25, 1976 and its birth recorded in Gegenschein 15, *Le Revue DoDo*, which was, in fact, a catalogue for this first in a long line of BIG PRODUCTIONS. The magazine had now been transformed into a 'live magazine,' the ultimate representation of the original intention of presenting the art of 'real, living people.' This 'first issue' presented a multiplicity of performance, entertainment and Art. Some of the artists who performed or displayed their art (in *Galerie DoDo*) were: Richard Kostelanetz (visual works + tape piece), William Packard (student readings from the Bible), Jane Goldberg (tap dancing), Jackson MacLow (visual works), Iris Lezak (paintings), Barbara Baracks (reading from novel), Sung (Jazz), N. Dodo Band's first public performance (H. & myself) and more.

For T and I, Art and Life had finally overlapped completely. We lived and worked in and for the *Placenter*, leaving a 'wide open space' (at the expense of a 'comfortable' living space) for the audiences we invited to our 'home' each week. Everything had become a performance. Just waking up in the *Placenter* was a performance. When we awoke we were instantly a part of the ongoing exhibit in *Galerie DoDo*.

The public performances were presented in series (*Fridays: On Your Mind, A Month of Sundays, Vaudeville of Aesthetics*) and took place weekly (and some with strength) for over a year. The artists who performed at *The Placenter* included musicians Jerome Cooper, Bob Moses, Steve McCall, Jay Clayton, Dave Van Tieghem, Antonio Zepeda, Billy Connors, The Acme Band (now The Breakfast Club) and the N. Dodo Band and writers/performers Fielding Dawson, Dick Higgins, Charles Bernstein, Yasunao Tone, Jeffrey Lohn, Kathy Acker (w/Peter Gordon), Ray DiPalma, Michael Lally, Bruce Andrews, Opal Nations, Jackson MacLow, Ascher/Straus, William Packard, Henry Korn, Matthew Paris, Stuart Sherman, the *Assembling* Mini

Avant Garde Festival, *Dramatika Magazine* Festival and *My Room On & Off* (w/David Herman and sets by Herm Freeman).

My works during this period were strongly conceptual and 'neoneo.' The 'Placenter of the City' was not unlike the 'academic womb' of 1972-74. I was once again living on the edge but protected by the art of (living) my life. I drove a cab to support my habit (of being an artist) and enjoyed being inside and outside and sitting still and still moving, simultaneously.

I also began developing some strong 'altered' egos like Stuart PP Tomatoz, F.W. Foolworth and Lydia Mellos, creating characters through which I could write and perform my life's fiction. I acted as their 'medium' which took many varied forms (painting, music, poetry, fictions, and performance).

Music was fast becoming the meeting place for all of my dabbles. H & I began to attract and take on (in a 'neoneo spirit') some additional band members. These were a combination of other 'musically inclined' artists and (to our surprise) 'real' musicians. What was once a theoretical 'band of artists' became an 8 piece jalopy with some 'real' commercial potential within the context of the 'new wave' scene in NYC. The *N. Dodo Band* grew and grew, playing all the local NYC and Jersey clubs, attracting and ultimately signing with a manager and a producton company and just missing signing a recording contract when it imploded and fell apart in 1979 (another BIG PRODUCTION) - *Todo el mundo es dodo!*

I made some new and lasting relationships at the *Placenter* and lost others. Dave Zimmer and Matty Paris (MONSTERS-IN-THE-CLOSET) joined forces with the *Placenter* and have continued to be two of my closest collaborators. Henry Korn and I became fast friends (unlike fast food we didn't devour each other) and H.F. (without whose help and support the *Placenter* may not have surfaced) continued as chief cohort.

By the summer of 1978 things were winding down. T left for a European vacation (for various reasons, one of which was our relationship) and I was tiring of the way I was now being viewed in relation to the *Placenter* which was, as a 'club owner.' Artists were beginning to treat me as if I were making money at 'their expense' which, in fact, was just the opposite. I was driving a cab and barely meeting the expenses of rent and promotion.

At the same time I met B.O., a woman who had just come to NY from Texas and, since T hadn't written once and had left my heart open to suggestion, B and I fell in love. It was a heartfelt decision that the *Placenter* was over and on September 25, 1978 the space was sold.

On October 9, 1978 while B and I were asleep in our new apartment on 14th St., the *Placenter* burned down. That was the end of that (period),

MY ROOM, OFF & ON
(a rambling soliloquy)

Welcome to my room. Here is where I live, off & on. These 'things' that surround me, that sit and reek from environment, are my drums, my source of percussion, what bangs when I activate, off & on.

For instance, if I had a repressed revelation stuck somewhere in the nowhere, I'd reach for this (*picks up a plunger*) and attack my frustration with great relish and suction.

(*He puts the plunger over his mouth and nose and presses it firmly while continuing to talk.*)

I concentrate on 'things' like constipation, jacks-in-the-box, springs, slinkies, potential energy, tugs-of-war, snorkels, snakes and coils *and* (*he slowly pulls the plunger from his face and he continues to speak but now in a 'possessed' voice*): I...am...the...crux...the...itch...of... consciousness...where it bends...and...takes...turns...being ...present...

(*he pauses to shake it off*)

Ahem. Well. That is the last resort just as I am at the point of no return, when I am 'off' so to speak...

(*he breaks off suddenly and loses the 'sound' of his words but he continues to speak in 'silence'*)

I eat in this room, off & on, keeping my NATURE NATURE and my HUMAN NATURE satisfied... (*sound returns to his words*) up front, beyond the questions and over and over and beyond the call of duty which sits in the middle of my body excreting autonomically to itself in silence. I eat this room, off & on and IT, me, on & off.

(*pause*)

I do this off & on. *(turns lights off & on)*
I do this on & off. *(turns radio on & off)*
I do this off & on. *(knocks object off the table and places it back on)*

(*pause*)

Everything in this room is done & not done, off & on, including me.

(*pause*)

This fiction, this giant gesture (*makes a 'tiny' gesture*), this overall off & on, represents and defines the structural sputtering of STRUCTURE and its 'retrospective' systems. Now you may ask, "how can he say that".....without the plunger. Well, it beats me, on & off.

(*pause*)

On & off this room tells me stories about the order of peace and the disorder of pieces. One night, on & off, I recorded one of these stories. Off & on I do this. (*turns tape recorder on*)

(*ROOM = tape recorder* on *with taped voice, HIM = tape recorder* off *with 'live' voice*)

ROOM: The trouble with this story
HIM: it began
ROOM: is in an adherence to disbelief caused solely by the concept of singularity.
HIM: it continued
ROOM: Once upon a time before the 'eyes' had it, the Simultaneous Consciousness was as intact as the spectrum
HIM: it paused
ROOM: and this is where it begins.
HIM: what begins?
ROOM: It. It. The struggle and the peace. And the pieces of the struggle. And the pieces of the peace. And It.

HIM: go on
ROOM: And God said 'let there be work and compensation and competition and mutations and lots of tongues, hordes of tongues and lips, lots of lips in formation, lots of words, lots of tongues, lots of information, lots of...'
HIM: it stopped abruptly and paused
ROOM: And once upon a time there *was* no room, just space and in it the most perfect and grandiose gesture imaginable. It could not be discerned by any of the 5 or 6 senses known to any living 'thing' or any 'thing' that was ON. It was the simultaneous breath of every 'thing' that was OFF. It was the great silver gesture of POTENTIAL. It was where the ego was a pup. And there was a great expectation that 'something just might happen.'
HIM: it is here where the room shifted.
ROOM: And since that time the clock has become kinetic and time marches on...
HIM: and OFF. (*turns recorder off*)

(*pause*)

Nonetheless this room serves no real purpose. But it does serve *that* purpose. On & off I have room to move, very rigidly and very seldomly.

(*he begins to dance very 'mechanically'*)

But it gives me a chance to glimpse at the laws of the Universe and laugh. Off & on I even get a chance to understand the intricate balances that pervade all the fallings down and risings up which simultaneously indicate the not so delicate imbalance that supports every theory. As a matter of fact, the 'glimpses' themselves seem to be the purest formulation of that 'not so delicate imbalance.'

(*pause*)

Off & on language also reflects this.

(*bursts out laughing*)

Excuse me but I just thought of something very funny.

(a brief pause for some 'mechanical' movement)

The space allotted to each person in a lifetime is limited to a very specific infinity whose exterior we never see. We carry these 'limited infinities' in a mysterious package, a room. A very abstract contra-diction is spoken in it. It is a room that contains all the space in the Universe and yet its miniscularity does not permit us to see it.

(He bursts out laughing and goes and sits with his back to the audience continuing to mumble and laugh to himself. After a time, he gets up and turns on *the television and watches it for a while. Then he gets up, turns the TV* off *and faces the audience. He begins to talk but he bursts out laughing, turns back to the TV, turns it* on *and sits back down with his back to the audience. After another short while he begins to get restless. He gets up, turns the TV* off *with a 'snap' and faces the audience. He begins to sob and fondle the 'things' in his room. Suddenly he grabs a favorite object and begins to scurry across the room screaming cliches like 'GOOD AS GOLD,' 'TIME IS ON MY SIDE,' IGNORANCE IS BLISS' etc. He eventually scurries into the 'Mysterious Package' and closes the lid.)*

THERE IS AN INTERMISSION HERE OF 5 MINUTES THAT IS 'ACTUALLY' TIMED AND WRITTEN OUT ON A BLACKBOARD. HE REMAINS IN THE MYSTERIOUS PACKAGE (BOX), FACING THE AUDIENCE. WHEN THE 5 MINUTES ARE UP HE BEGINS TO TALK FROM INSIDE THE MYSTERIOUS PACKAGE.

So you see there is no such thing as *further* studies. We can never get to that point. The Universe is so overpowerfully small and that apparent incongruity is born out of the infinite limitations of this very room. That's what is going on & off. And that's what we can and can't see.

(After a short pause he gets out of the mysterious package and walks over to the TV and turns it on *and returns, nonchalantly, to the inside of the mysterious package. He soon begins to laugh hysterically and then begins to make quiet, bizarre sounds. Suddenly he leaps from the mysterious package and slams it down with a powerful vengeance. He turns to the audience, slowly 'loosening' his rigid body as he turns. When he is fully facing them he is smiling and he very suavely ambles over to his dressing mirror and begins to remove his 'casual' attire. Underneath his 'casual' attire he has on a pair of 'dress' pants and a 'dress' shirt. He whistles while he 'un' dresses, and while he painstakingly ties his tie in a very 'carefully chaotic' knot, he begins to speak, almost in a sing-song.)*

I'm right and I'm wrong. I'm right and I'm left. I'm up and I'm down. I'm in and I'm out. I'm right and I'm wrong.

(He stands back from the mirror, admires himself, nods his approval and then sits down to put on his sneakers. After his sneakers are on he begins to polish them with shoe polish and continues talking.)

The space in which we grow disappears on the day we are born. That day was a kinetic culmination of a universe of potential. And since that day we all take turns standing still, still moving and moving still, up a ladder of myths and mysteries, on our way somewhere. Life is, after all, terminally off & on. We fill up the space, the time, with activity (*parallel to gravity*), a kinetic response to our own limited potential (*on*). We move within our confinements, our cells, like oxidation, burning (*off*) the foundation of our support. We eat ourselves up, (*pause*) pause, (*pause*) and regenerate.

(He gets up and walks over to his chair, turns and gives the audience a friendly smile. He walks over and turns on the TV and it is a 'live' video shot of the audience. He sits in his chair with his back to the audience watching the monitor of the audience watching him. This continues until the last person in the audience leaves the theatre)

Herm Freeman

THE AUTOMYTHOLOGY OF PHIL DEMISE

1. in the mood for accidental methods"
shooting up
through the floor

the occurrent fetish oxidizes itself
makes footprints in the invisible concrete
washes its vapor and remembers itself to the family

"there is no escaping it
shoots up
through the floor
through the cracks in its own outline
making its way towards the heart
of the matter

2. where there is no premise, demise appears
not as
the premise
but as
a loosely violated
promise

hopping from no premise to no premise
hoping for an acute attack of substance
getting further and further
close"

3. as in journey
as in all journals
it begins forever never ending
on time,"
a cloud of dust
and a haha

4. "getting off the land for a moment,
I could see the distraction clearly"

at a loss for the word
for it
escapes me
I huddle
in its corner
"its corner travels through me like blood

5. just to fill the space
and make it appear, is not enough
"but sufficient

THE CURRENT SITUATION

with the overcoat slung   over
                                        the electronic skeleton
begging for skin
              for five, "slap me five"
              recognize my substance

              simply

give it a moment's notice   like a bolt
                                        out of the black

    a bolt with speed
    a bullet
    with a vanilla latch
    invisibly secure

I am waiting and the trees wait with me and we are naked

                                        somehow
                                        the sky
         is no umbrella
the sun
no solace
         me
         no
              unit
                                   yet continuance
                                   backs up the psychic glass
                                   like silver foil
                                   slipped between the discs
and the current
situation reflects the exactness of mistakes

THE AMERICAN EVOLUTION

deep in the wood of night
the juxtaposition fits
into its mother's slip
and slips out
near the water's edge
permitting the moon
to bay at the ocean
and the bay
to moon the beach
and further along
the chain
the concrete weeps

PRODUCTION LINES

as the morning sets its yellow teeth
into new york's short black breath
the sleeping asphalt buckles
with oceanic noise

like giant breakers
trucks wash ashore
filled with enticing sharks

the public pulls its eye
from the telescope
seeking the affirmation
of its sleep

it echoes from the back
of rectangular semis

it skips off the pages
of television

it sneaks out
from the opening of locks

it blossoms
from small talk

it jumps out
from the horizon

and in the human factor
a chaotic mixture
not unlike a speck of galaxy
constructs a tree
out of concrete
makes ridiculous extensions
of itself
and works for a crack
at possession

there is no escape
from new york
its ego bolts itself
to your brain

an awesome shadow
of the miracle

a symbiotic parasite
nesting in your consciousness

an ocean floor
without water

an ocean
of oxygen

a thirsty rock

A BOMB

out the window onto the exquisite black cement
city nights buckling with the strained clamor
of muffled diversity and whispering colors
upwards of 8 million inching toward my window
rising from the city's cracks like an ocean
of rivers rising off the face of a concept
inching toward my window with an army of secret lips
invisibly shouting commands and kissing trees

such epitome!   my atoms split/

THE FALL OF THE STATE OF THE EMPIRE

it moves through the rainbow like a leaf
and more so in the city like a rock
especially on the alternate sides
where the window begins its false view
I take exception, I take lots of exceptions
I move them from place to place
expecting some sudden windfall
a drop of air dripping off a leaf
itself dropping off a tree
in fall
waiting with open arms
locked to my shoulder
to catch a glimpse
and quickly retire

IN THE MEANTIME

a new skyline scribbles across a glass leaf
jumping through perspectives, a lion
jamming the spectrum with mesmerized tones
the flipside of an octagon
absorbed in three dimensions
on third avenue
not to mention the drifting silence
sliding downtown through the staggered light

NEW YORK DADA

there is a dada in each of us
and some are MOTHERS
big gaping tomatoes
arbitrarily red and its opposite
kookoo

and you stand on one finger
in your office overlooking
the possibility of break away
speed

making personal contact
with strangers and the strangest
things

simply walking back simply
through this city
with bucks in your pockets
and clowns in your cheeks

chuckling

MATHEMATIC OF TWO FIGURINES

1.
This is the middle of it, the middle of it, intricate and dense, intricate and dense loose ends, loose ends comb the thick follicles, the thick follicles in search of a neat package.

In the distance, unknown factors, unknown factors lie awake, lie awake in a blinking eye, in a blinking eye irritated by the dust, by the dust of termination.

Two erratic figurines embrace each other, embrace each other in this, in this torrential mathematic, this torrential mathematic openly hostile, openly hostile to the space between, to the space between two numbers, between two numbers surrendering to the force, to the force of subtraction, the force of subtraction and equality.

These two, one by one, expect logic, expect logic to imagine, to imagine its own result.

Automatically they promise each other, they promise each other heaven, they promise each other heaven and whisper, and whisper through their secret, erect bodies, through their secret bodies bending, bending through the stacks of curvatures, the stacks of curvatures and projections.

The comma that separates their lives, their lives separate from their future, their future in the numerals of calculus, in the numerals of calculus the mathematic circulates and divides, the mathematic circulates and divides their lives into fractions, into fractions of secrets.

These two, one by one, sanction their escape into each other, into each other with invisible fantasies, invisible fantasies riding up the roots of fresh flowers, the roots of fresh flowers rising into their tongues.

In their own words they speak in unison, in unison they trap the universe in syllables, the universe in syllables tumbling over the thick follicles like tears, the thick follicles like tears tremble in the dark light, in the dark light shimmering pearls flex their ivory and fall asleep, and fall asleep on a pillow of possibilities.

2.
"Pardon me dear shadow, dear shadow where is the substance, the substance that eclipsed infinity, that eclipsed infinity and retained your dimensions, your dimensions gasping for flesh and bones, flesh and bones to hang a skin of depth, to hang a skin of depth around your flat mirage?"

"There are no shadows in this mathematic, this mathematic is more or less, more or less the idea of a shadow, the idea of a shadow you can multiply, a shadow you can multiply with ideas."

He lights a cigarette and leans back, leans back against the opposing view.

"Then what is the source of this shadow, this shadow of ideas, ideas which pass through my system, through my system into your shadow, into your shadow and through the random figures of your shape?"

She steps off the pedestal and walks toward the door, the door that leads away, that leads away into the idea of privacy, the idea of privacy that separates the men from the women, the women from the shadows.

"I cannot accept this," he whispers, he whispers within a pastel consciousness, a pastel consciousness flushed with spurts of deep red.

Being minus one accentuates the imbalance, the imbalance of the nature, the nature of two, one by one, one by one this mathematic adds up, this mathematic adds up to nothing, nothing in particular.

"I will call you in the morning, in the morning we will no longer be divided, be divided by this long, narrow division."

She nods a bewildered acceptance, a bewildered acceptance opens the door, the door opens and she vanishes, she vanishes into the shadows, the shadows huddled in the night.

3.

"Hello, this is me, this is me and the morning, the morning that holds our future in its clock, the clock that eventually catches up, that eventually catches up to the skeleton of our fleeing dreams, the skeleton of our fleeing dreams circling the backdrop of our face."

"What number do you want, do you want this number, this number that runs the gamut of peripheries, peripheries skirting the circumference with parenthetical remarks, remarks about the nature of couplets, of couplets marching up the vertical axis, up the vertical axis and into the relativity of deep space?"

"Yes I want this number, this number that vibrates in the electrons of your voice, the electrons of your voice that beckon my unresolved circuits, circuits that seek further additions, further additions that keep me awake, that keep me awake in my dreams."

The silence at the other end makes him wonder, makes him wonder if she can still be, if she can still be counted on, still be counted on and be still, and be still at the same time, at the same time that he is waking up.

"Are you still there, there in the vision of you still being there, still being there in the silence which you speak so well?"

The lack of answers click, answers click in, click inside his head that aches, his head that aches with silence.

Herm Freeman

TCHOUKI DEMURE

we seem to be walking on matchsticks
up a mountain
but a red, red heat
yeah, the hot chuckle

an ancient patio disappeared
into a high staircase
in your woolly locks

white washed eternity rocketed
over the skyline
the white hot tips of the shake
and the lash of the diamond
heads locked together

a syrupy gash on your arm
gray matter collapsed
and we looked in that dark place

was round like the moon
shaven sculptured features
and a rhythm of pelvic flesh

and then, oh
Like a wing

in between your wheels lies a circle
in that space a room develops
the ins and outs spit fire
lions jump through the hoops
a cage walks out of your mouth
a cannon shoots the audience a great distance
you fly into the fog with bright eyes

LOVE

just the idea of it!
reciprocating and absorbing
a blue-white bolt of water
a cold dry liquid floats deep
within the core of human electricity
love comes in many frequencies
and hobbles through a burst of speed
entering the spine of batteries
through a hole in the head

I succumb to it briefly all the time
letting its special pulse control
my circulation and its current bullets
to invade my pistol with milk

what a sucker for love!

it extends itself through the wire
out into a broken clock
the limp hands cover the six
the tick tock echoes in silent explosions
the flow is an endless package of light
a mirror filled with primitive reflections
backing up into the sack

the idea of it excites me!

she is the definitive abstraction
an angle measured with bent protractors
plugged into eye sockets like a flower
she reminds me of some intangible display
fire crackling through a forest of leaves
in the not too distant future

I burn for the security of her circuits!

generations and regenerations eat breakfast
with this wet dream cell
making breath a prisoner of the lung
and the heart a simple drum
played by children with numb hands
and sticks and stones

Oh what a good idea!
what a delicious transference!
what a hot continuum!

THIS LESS THAT PLUS IT

this long poem is about
the fact that I am
never

a pause separates
and changes

the elements
are flying

down the gullet of concepts
the negative chamber

in the reversal of heart
there are no objectives

clamoring for certainty
and certainly exist in false
notions

of time and subtraction there
of

It

perhaps It is my favorite word
and It is perhaps
without doubt
the most

and underneath it all
deep down
through the crux
of shadows

the square root
of which

I am
is

a factor

I am
minus magic

without the power
to transform
or generate

without the force
to explode

It

It, the transition
It, like the tree,
like me,
changing colors,
falling

rain, falling
in the body
of the brain

I am
not

myself

FREQUENTLY REAL

the soft thud of ideas
landing in the pocket of the mitt
in the midst of a dumb ear
colors fan across the eye socket
and they are frequently real
without me, I am it

the overwhelming package of pieces
things offer in deep analysis
the morsels of invisible traces
the bolting velocity of paralysis
and above all it is wholly possible
without me, it is

all things have a tendency
leaning out of its particles
a thousand options for ascendency
and one stiff icicle
liquid, solid and with good reason
without me, it is me

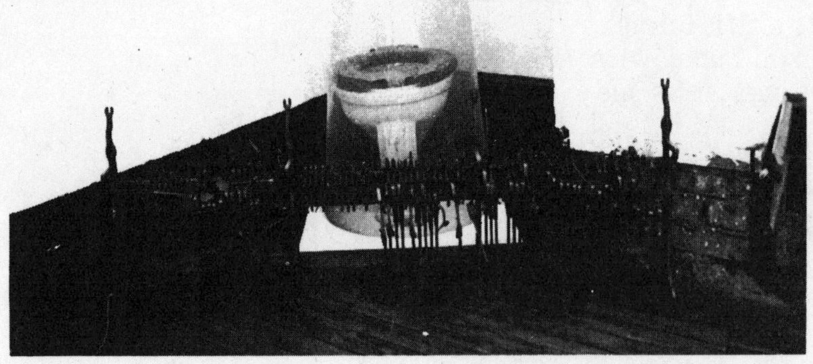

A John Cage Stuart P.P. Tomatoz

AVANT IT ALL
toward a prenatal civilization

PREPHASE

I have many fantastic fantasies and one hard clump of real shit. One is the mountain and one is the river and I am stumped. Direction is my appendage making natural moves behind my back. I am the package being delivered. If such lack of control is my controlling factor how am I to decide which religion best fits my rut and will least disturb my unevenness?

My innate, astronomical intelligence tells me that there is no way to be sure. Existence comes as it always came, out of a chance blending whose only laws are its present form, and then only deciphered later at the convenience of retrospect. We are continuously following the bread crumbs back to our origen which is a black pit of stars hanging on the edge. And this Origen is infinitely present in the electricity of our existence at the same time that we are walking back home and calling it future.

There is no prophet or profit of the future, we can only predict what we already know, and what we don't know is our future. This moving paradox can only be enjoyed if thoroughly believed.

Here's to your past, may it be bright and cheery. Because what I secretly believe, I believe everyone secretly believes, which is that what they secretly believe, they believe everyone secretly believes and we do, and we are all right and all doomed by our own egos. We, that is, you and I will only survive our own lifetimes.

UNLIKE:

to formulate, to create, to realize, to make,
to change dimensions, to rearrange, to title,
to organize, to rehearse, to lie, to perfect,

the simple truth about extensions
defined by the inability to measure the molecules in an
idea
the stupid self claiming credit for found objects
and extending them through high and mighty erections
where you kneel before your self and beg for success

unlike the tree

*****

in absolution
a line's direction is directly proportional
to the environment that surrounds its movement

to go forward, to go backward, to revolve
to go up, to go down, to go off,

all brief skeletons
jumping off the deck of a sinking ship

unlike sparks

*****

Avant it all.
Avant all directions.
Avant the derriere.
Avant all abstractions to meet their makers.
Avant God.
Avant retrospect and the ridiculous.
Avant logical chance.
Avant mistakes and missed cues.
Avant maybe.
Avant acceptance and its zen dada duties.
Avant failure to succeed and fail.
Avant mutts, boobs, and hybrids.
Avant pitfalls and risings.
Avant pity and privacy.
Avant high performance.
Avant special conditions.
Avant proportions equal to the period.
Avant plant life and confidence.
Avant nothing.
Avant fragrances and their shadows.
Avant the negative.
Avant it all.

*****

there is something to be said for it
for it all,

and it is better left
unsaid, unaided

unlike an emergency

*****

a wind blows through the chamber
the particles it carries and accumulates
dictate the next inch with varied precision
until I fall into line
unlike the ethereal.

forever meaningless, forever yellow
washing an ocean away with the ease
of a river and returning at the same
speed in no time.

frequently a visitor, frequently the vista
edging along the edge unlike a snake
sinking and rising to the surface,
a rubber edge that bends with the matter
that hits it and bounces back with a
whooshing snap unlike concrete.

a black pit of stars hanging on the edge
our origen, our end.

*****

the middles. who suffers from the middles un
like I do?

*****

Avant it all.
Avant middles and their pink counterparts.
Avant babies.
Avant falling, to continue, to rise.
Avant spelling.
Avant panties and breathless anticipation.
Avant clear cuts.
Avant marching on backwards.
Avant tiptoes.
Avant it all.

STUART PP TOMATOZ

Stuart PP Tomatoz was born in Rome in 1918 to Dada and Mama Tomatoz. In 1933 he was forced to flee from the Swiss because they could not stand the presence of anything more neutral than they were. He settled in New York City where he edited the obscure magazine EGO in which he published only his own work. In 1952 he had his first TWO MAN SHOW at the infamous Black Gallery. In 1957 Tomatoz withdrew from the arena of Public Art and returned to Italy where he continued to conceive until his timely death in 1965. It was reported that when he died he was semi-conscious. He was buried in Rome under the epitaph he himself had written in 1916:

WHAT'S UP?

(this short biography was written by Tomatoz himself sometime before his death)

Tomatoz Pulling Clouds Out of Tomatoes Herm Freeman

THIS is the TITLE to TITLE

"Anything you claim TITLE to is art because you created the possession"

-stuart pp tomatoz,
spoken in soliloquy-

TITLES to pieces in the PIECE ENTITLED : THIS is the TITLE to *TITLE:*

1. THIS is the TITLE to *TITLE*
2. UP ON OPENING (in conjunction with Performance de Resistance performed by Phil Demise and based on a Tomatoz concept)
3. CHAIR WITH EYES LOOKING AT IT
4. PLANT ENTRANCED
5. FLOOR BOARD BORED WITH FLAWS
6. POLISH
7. EMBELLISHED
8. FANCY WIND POTENTIAL
9. DO OR
10. in KITSCH in

"Language claims title to things and they are inseparable"

*****

The piece THIS is the TITLE to *TITLE* is a realization of a Tomatoz concept from his manuscript entitled: ENTITLED: THIS is the TITLE to *TITLE* of the BOOK OF CONCEPTS/ NEATNESS DOESN'T COUNT. HONK IF YOU ARE LYDIA MELLOS & A JOHN CAGE are also pieces based on a Tomatoz concept in that manuscript which reads: *"All things have names, all names have things attached to them. In this piece the participant comes upon a name and then sets out to find the thing it is attached to."*

This is the Title to Title

In this piece the participant actually draws on the connections between the person, the environment and the language which are the elements of the Situation.

the participant claims Things in the environment and takes Title to them through a relationship to Language.

the Titles should be placed in the environment unobstrusively and no one need be told where they lie (or tell the truth).

the connections are always there but the possession of them is a creation.

I claim this Piece under the Title: This is the Title to Title.

Tomatoz circa 1960

How Franklin left the restaurant. How he struts with menu. How he chooses and breaks bread. How he taunts expectancy. This they acknowledge. This they turn heads about. This they draw conclusions on their napkins. This they whisper to their neighbors. When Franklin left the restaurant. When he struts with menu. When he chooses and breaks bread. When he taunts expectancy. Why they acknowledge. Why they turn heads about. Why they draw conclusions on their napkins. Why they whisper to their neighbors. This Franklin knows. How Franklin knows. This they know. It was 12:20 when Franklin left the restaurant.

THE POLITICS OF INEXPERIENCE

the politics of inexperience   and the repressed obsessions
this   and   the progress of reaction

the nervous disorder   and   the corporate entity
this   and   the inhibition of prohibition

the probability of possibility   and crystal clear indecision
this   and   perhaps certainly

the shedding of *the*   and   not *and* but is additional
this   and   that   and   more

the complex of simplicity   and   urgent pauses
this   and   the dimensions of always

the unknown repetitions

TIME BY ANY OTHER NAME
(Still takes Time)

Last year instead of a clock we had twelve geese.
This year instead of the geese we have tomatoes.
The impact of time was the same in both years
but this year we had more spaghetti.

Last year instead of seasons we had four arguments.
This year instead of arguments we have toilets.
The impact of the weather was the same in both years
but this year we held less in.

This time last year it was 12-1/2 geese and I didn't
think it was such a good idea.

ENST

eastern non standard time runs five minutes earlier than eastern standard time the advantages of such a wide eyed system are much too numerous to name like being there before you arrive how nice it is to see you before you come

next paragraph

DECOMPOSITIONS

This is the procession of decompositions.
The unoriginal pleasure and sin.
Me as overlap.
The anarchy of substance.
Me on top of It.
Who I am, ridiculous.
And It which is Them.
Which is It.
Which is which.
Mutually.
Slabs of minutes.
Slabs of seconds.
Slabs of thirds.
Slabs of links.
Slabs of theories.
Slabs of aesthetics.
Slabs of disappearance.
This is also what that which was is when it was original.

f.w. foolworth

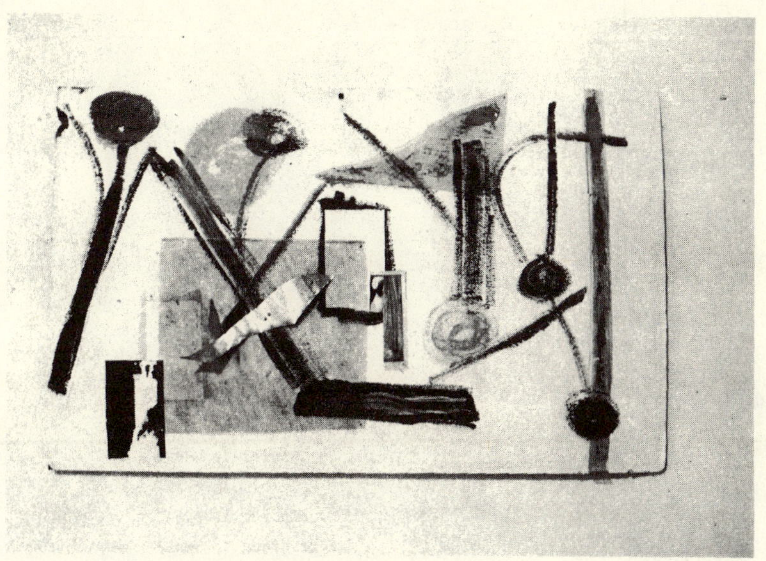

doing does not necessarily lead to done
and does not really matter what's done is done
and how it is is doing well no matter what

F. W. Foolworth

what does a dodo do?
a dodo does it all
todo, everything
making a big todo
about nothing, nada
a dada doing
but building and doing
what it has to do,
todo and nada
and do do it
until it is almost
all done
and then,
oddly,
doing it
again
this time
without wings
without odd moods
without gods
but doing what a dodo does
and doing it, well
almost doing it well

DODO
Raphus cucullatus
30" tall 46lbs
Extinct, ca 1693
Warning: The Surgeon General Has Determined
That Extinction Is Dangerous to Your Health.

Phil Demise

JET BLACK JET

for Bruce and Ellen Hutchinson

the little sky unaddressed its cloud with a vast blue shrug.
the blue itself arrived in dribs and drabs, seeping through
the jet black network. an army of wet blue dropping from
the camouflage of an infinite, thick darkness, settling into
an invisible head of air. a light black dome, a topical tank
filled with fish sperm and fleshy comas, quickly
moving slowly into sleep.

and so the atmosphere packs a few rods and speckled birds
for the cohesion of dreams. and the little sky blankets
the fish from a multitude of cosmic hooks. and the
sparkling question marks are too mysterious to pass
through the mesh, and too real to be caught asleep.

a shrug, and the colors juggle their frequencies, shifting
slightly into major structures. simultaneously, the little
sky in our headache breathes heavily on a cloud. and a
swarm of jet black buries its dust in the blue.

DUSK DREAM

the dickens from one person
and the willies from another
meet on two abandoned parabolas
at the moment of disconnection
a herd of white ponies gallop up
in a steel plated theorem
making sounds like black ponies
((enough of this))
then the multicolored twerps
collide in an atmosphere of lemon
and go back home to the bone heap

DON'T BELIEVE THIS

for Jeffrey Lohn

the emptiness that precedes emptiness
glowing at the tip of bee stings
if the proper application eats the atmosphere
and removes the milk from goat's eyes

the terminal accident
the life force *for no reason*

and that is definitely 6 or 7 tomatoes
and that is definitely not them
and here is where we differ
and close
for openers
that is definitely 6 or 7 tomatoes

MIS
NEONEO IS DADA^SPELLED DIFFERENTLY

and then the line drive base hit
and the spitfire jet
percussing to the midst
of conjunctive crashes
leading into peripheral damage
and the jacket's zipper
and the stampede of canaries

seventeen tweets

and the stampede of canaries
and then the line drive base hit

THE SAVIORS OF ROCK N ROLL

THE

N. DODO BAND

Herm Freeman

THE CREATURE OF HABIT

the hands of the little clock in my battery are tied
it has been kicked out of my head, the pupil
a sudden puff of renegade electricity
charging little headless electrons
through the wireless space of transition

the external collapse of habits and comfort
pass through the membrane of my shadow
projected by the sun's light and the future
onto the hot concrete of a vision

I'm only human,
nothing more

all the cracks in the continuity are chuckling
a few deserted dreams suck on the truth
all the landscapes and cliches echo
in an avalanche of snowballs

the creature of habit crawls through the ice
with fire in its eyes

OTHERWISE

bashed quality
exboned grip unhitched

IT
firm needs (form)

cry cat
scaredy baby

meaning empty eggs empty meaning eggs

AND
DNA

altitudinal

high cheek rustling
sashay milk branch

crescento

homogenized straps)   homosap cowbell

bristle ice beating on the tourist more than once
bristle ice beating on the tourist more than twice

dioxyribonucleic etc

THIS POEM

This poem is about *this poem*
as all poems are even if they
are not this one. But all poems
that are thought to be poems
are not all like this poem which
happens to be about *this poem*
as all poems are even if they
are not this one. Not all poems
that are thought to be poems
are poems about those poems as
this one is about *this poem*
and nothing else which is not
this poem. But this thing about
which this poem flies is not
just anything. It is *this thing*
that it is about. And this thing
is this poem as all poems are
even if they are not this poem.

FRAGMENTS

The sky is dark and precipitates shadows in my eyes. There is no narration for fragments. They appear and disappear before the language gathers coherency in its syntax. They mean something for a moment and then crash their points against a wall of sparks. At best you can smell them or taste the yellow-orange perhaps of their after image.

DEVICES

To refrain from adultery is a device. To abstain from intoxication is a device. To let go of our grip is a device. To not commit murder is a device.

I don't want to continue along those lines yet I want this thing to go on. I'm not through but I'm through with that.

Maybe I am though.

I am.

SADDLE SOARS

the true nature of existence has no extremes
it is all a dense mid drift
being pressed by two dark gloves
filled with wind
the ends justify the middle
the tendency to burst
becomes the overriding motion
and the saddle
soars

so many birdbrains
instruct us to eat heartache
our teeth cut into the matter
and break apart
our bodies syncopate
in a masked huddle
while the horse
of a different color
disappears entirely
into the shade
of weightlessness

we kick our hiding
with the spur of the moment
we kick it
until the beast gallops
through the face
of an empty clock
bucking the whole picture
which developed in no time
and waits in the dark room
just above the sky

we are saddled
with a human,
being human

THE FOREST IN THE DEPTH OF FIELDS

1.
in the forest
in the depth of fields
a distance flowers
attracts a closet
full of yellow jackets
each informally dressed
each whispering
a particle of buzz

2.
I hear the incredible hum
though inaudible
I hear it humming

3.
a seven inch cloud
separates the perfect (-)
ion
from its blue bed
drifting in
like a sudden sting

4.
antelopers
through a range
of colors
occupying the shadows

5.
the full force of wild life
splashes off the canyon
echoing the ring of raindrops
aching to evaporate
backing up into weightlessness

6.
I give it some thought
and the clarity attacks
the opaque landscape
with translucence

7.
I'm not too bright
the inherent must burst
explode like a memory
sink its fire into my vision
before I see the incredible red

8.
in this music
a cacophony sucks in
its stomach
folding the dissonance

9.
a machine
leaping from its gears
a habit
twisting its own head off

10.
I can no longer stop
the assigned delineation
has dissolved
into the aroma of depth

11.
changed its tune

PRECIPICE AT THE HEIGHT OF GLORY

The one dimensional wind which casts no shadow
and the four dimensional sky whose shadow we are
whose shadow we are which casts no shadow
whose orbit crashes through the substance of this world
whose shadow is lost in the shadow of art and galaxies

What is the thing whose shadow is the universe?

Being a shadow, we have nothing to fear
but sounds vanishing into thin air, dark space,
whose sound is the sound we are, which is no sound
in the dark, in the diminishing light of dead stars
years prior to their death, prior to their shadows
whose shadow we are which casts no shadow no sound
no shadow swelling in the solution and dissolution
alternately like the current source of light
of shadow

Herm Freeman

COME SEE COME

the glass bells prevent
the collapse
necessary for the mad dash
they ring in closets
I live in the pouch
of an icicle
dripping with disappearance
opening candles
with water falls
the perspective
cuts through
cracks
up the middle
with a dull blade
separating
the milk from its glass
the sleep from its river
the sky from its sky
the tight lips
from the mouth of dreams

meanwhile
back in the shrinking spike
the obvious blurs
emphasizing the soft overlap
of delineation
crystalizing
the delirium
outlining
the proper coagulation
of fantasy

one is alone
in one's own
dream

I am in a kind of translucent packing-case, possibly made of plastic, in the midst of interplanetary space; I am sitting in it with my legs stretched out, naked, tiny, the size of a five- or six-year-old child; in front of me is another child, in the same position, who looks like my twin; is he my double?

Eugene Ionesco

Herm Freeman

14th STREET B.T.
(Before Tristan)
October 1978-February 1981
New York City

14th St. BT (Before Tristan) - October 1978 - March 1981

I was relieved that my life was shifting. B & I found a comfortable apartment (semi-middle class) on 14th Street off Third Ave. I welcomed the smaller more personal size of my new home in comparison to the 'barely' essential, wide open space of the *Placenter*. I also welcomed the release from the pressures of coordinating and producing a 'scene' and looked forward to concentrating my attentions on my own artistic future which at this time was almost entirely linked to the future of the *N. Dodo Band.*

B and I were married in November of 1978 and spent the next 2 1/2 years excitedly working on numerous projects which each yielded its own kind of success.

First was the *N. Dodo Band.* It was during 1979 that the Band almost made its absurd mark. We had painstakingly evolved into a real entity, a real product. We tried hard to (and almost could) perform the music 'well' but it seemed only at the expense of 'true'. We could never quite reconcile our 'un-musicality' with our dream of perfection.

The Band's message was mixed and simultaneous which was only a reflection of the band's actual makeup - 8 quirky individuals with no 'recognized' leader (though it was my assumed position). Some were 'artists' and some were not and some were musicians and some were not. Some were responsible and some were not. We were, in fact, a 'living' example of 'neoneo anarchy,' a microcosm of a world based on simultaneous differences and needs. Our main weakness was our lack of both confidence and common ground which was also an unrecognized strength. If we had recognized, accepted and respected our dissonances, we could have used that tension as a power, as a tool. Instead, since not everyone was capable of understanding the philosophical possibilities, we acted and reacted as if each individual were a territory and it became the operative to defend one's position. Pretension overshadowed the tension and our power dissipated until we finally collapsed.

As the *Dodo Band* soared to unheard of heights of extinction, B and I continued our own personal projects. B began her documentary on the *N. Dodo's* emergence and ultimate decline ("Drop From The Top"). She filmed (in 16mm) concerts, management meetings, rehearsals, fan reactions and our own 'high' hopes. In 5 months we shot over 4000 feet of film which remains in the can, uncut.

At the same time (with B's help) I edited Gegenschein's most adventuresome issue to date - The BIG RED 161718. It was almost 300 pages of some of our most important contemporary writers including Tristan Tzara, Kenneth Patchen, Dick Higgins, Richard Kostelanetz, Opal Nations and Guy Beining. Also included, bound into the issue, was an historical catalog of Gegenschein's publications and productions. To celebrate the publication of this issue B & I produced yet another show. This BIG PRODUCTION was held at St. Clement's Church and included numerous live performances and the showing of some rare Dada/Surrealist films on loan from MOMA (though the issue, itself, did not make an appearance).

Shortly after Gegenschein 161718 appeared we began our short-lived book series, THE NOTBOOK SERIES. We published 5 small books (*From the Desk of Dr. Know* by Henry Korn, *Ice Rescue Station* by Guy Beining, 2 books by myself, *Maninfested* and *White Rushes* and *Red Rice* by Yuki Hartman (which was pulled at the last minute because of an aesthetic disagreement).

I also began running a reading series at the Viridian Gallery on 57th St. with Dave Zimmer which I dropped soon after its inception because it tasted too much like the *Placenter* experience.

Meanwhile, the *Dodo Band* rose into the ranks of reality and most of my time was spent negotiating contracts and producing Dodo myths and promotion (including 3 issues of a single sheet newspaper called *The Daily Dodo*). The band, however, was slowly disintegrating from the inside out based on mistrust and ego-centricities. After our *N. Dodo* extravaganza (*For Our Own Benefit* exhibition and performances) held at *The Space*, where we exhibited paintings and drawings by H.F., showed slides and films of Dodo concerts, read poetry and performed our songs, the internal combustion was getting too hot to handle.

In late 1979, I along with two other key members H.F. and J.K., quit the *Dodos* and began a more manageable, more easily controllable project, *Didus and the Fabulous Mascarenes* (named after the Dodo's latin name and the Islands from which it came and ultimately disappeared). We immediately came out with our own record (*So & So* b/w *These Boots Are Made For Walkin'*) on my own Xtinct Records label. This was *my* band but the 'neoneo' dream of a non-judgmental corporation of differences had been put to sleep by the distant rumblings of possible success.

This band came even closer to succeeding than N. Dodo but it too eventually split asunder under its own weight (wait). In September 1983 we gave what was to become our 'swan' concert in Central Park, as the finale of NYC's first (and only) *Art Parade* (produced by Henry Korn).

I wrote more than 75% of all the material the *N. Dodo Band* performed throughout its many incarnations and all the material performed by *Didus*. The songs ranged from conceptual to abstract to absurd to 'quirky commercial' and in some way tried to exemplify 'the ridiculous situation that is serious.'

I wrote most of the music on guitar (more precisely on 'gutar,' my own brand of percussive strumming and open G tuning) with the lyrics emanating from some spontaneous vocalization or from poems previously written and then stretched, bent and cut to fit into an improvised melody. The bands (mostly H.F. and J.K.) then provided an arrangement from an infinite number of choices. I was and still am a musical 'naif' and a 'primitif' virtuoso, leaving me free from the shackles of any particular system and enabling me to make some interesting leaps into the unknown. As a result, my songs and compositions were always a little (if not a lot) off center and though they sometimes seemed to tickle the visions of commercial recording moguls, they never captured their complete attention ($).

In the Winter of 1978, my book (letterpress pamphlet) WHAT I DON'T KNOW FOR SURE (Burning Deck, Providence R.I.) finally appeared after a year's preparation and marked my first book publication outside of my own press. It was an inspiration to me since I had always admired (and still do) the quality of production and material that is so carefully and tastefully presented by Keith and Rosmarie Waldrop.

My writing of this period still embraced the *Dada/Dodo* spirit. I began to see threads of history that very clearly linked my intuitions to those of the personages who presently interested me. In some cases they almost matched, word for word. Though I found myself linked to the past, my present was less cohesive, having to compete with the lure of a commerciality that was nibbling at my musical fronts. The 'business' of the bands and the overriding of my deep seated (seeded) *neoneo* attitude threw my 'art' for a loop.

Unlike other periods where the writing wrote itself, now I had to remind myself. I made up exercises to keep the 'deeper' me from atrophying while I pursued the real world. I used other 'art' as a point of departure (and arrival). On and off I made believe I was keeping a diary; I wrote a screenplay based on Harry Crosby's biography *Black Sun* and, along with D.Z., invented the *Dodoist Hordes* project (which appears in *Gegenschein 161718*). In general, I forced myself to express the simple movements that were still buried under layers of complex emotions. This method has, and continues to be in my employ to this very day (and is very much a part of why I am putting together this book and writing these introductions).

For the nine months of July 1980 through March 1981 I was preparing myself for a new life. Being a father was a complete unknown. Once again I was going to enter a new period and once again I was entering it as a primitive. I had no idea how it was going to change my life but I was certain it was. I looked forward to the change. And best of all it was at the root, at the deepest point of *neoneo*. A child was the ultimate creative act, a living, growing conception, the purest form of 'art as life' (life as art).

Tristan arrived on the afternoon of March 3, 1981 and on that same evening I recorded one of my most 'promising' songs, DEEP LOVE, written for my then pregnant wife and unborn child: "*Deep love can't be denied, a piece of sleep along a bumpy ride.*"

It was a new beginning and in the beginning there were beginnings and ends (period),

Herm Freeman

A TRAIN OF THOUGHT

neoneo

I have no philosophy. I believe in the oneness of two and three and four and minus five. The state of Art is New Jersey. A garden of assembly line illiteracy. It is read on the faces. It is embarrassing.

richter

Thus we let sense escape into the realm of nonsense, although it never left that of the senses. It drives us to the fragmentation or destruction of all artistic forms, and to rebellion for rebellion's sake; to an anarchistic negation of all values, a self exploding bubble, a raging *anti, anti, anti* linked with an equally passionate *pro, pro, pro*!

dada

ART falls asleep. ART needs an operation. ART is a pretension, warmed by the diffidence of the urinary tract. Thought is produced in the mouth.

neoneo

I am speechless. Forever holding my tongue. Uttering possibilities to the mindless judge sitting on a throne in my brain. Casting multitudes of fishy conclusions into my throat. I am a horse. I am a horse of a different color. I shoot horse and fly off into the sun on its bullet proof wings. High as the kite I was told to go out and fly, on a windless day.

arp

(Thus you see that one doesn't consume one's pater except slice by slice, it's impossible to do it in a single picnic and even the lemon falls to its knees before the beauty of nature.)

marinetti

When we feel a piece of iron we say: This is iron; we satisfy ourselves with a word and nothing more. Between iron and hand a conflict of preconscious force-thought-sentiment takes place. Perhaps there is more thought in the fingertips and the iron than in the brain that prides itself on observing the phenomenon.

If you've heard the sound of one hand, prove it. Without a word, thrust one hand forward.

gadji beri bimba glanddridi laula lonni cadori

grimbasa cundoma gridgicoma anoni leapa cambric
And perhaps is my favorite word.

The state of society is incontestably artificial; the power of one man over another must be always derived from convention or from conquest; by nature we are equal.

I smash drawers, those of the brain and those of social organization; everywhere to demoralize, to hurl the hand from heaven to hell, the eyes from hell to heaven, to set up once more, in the real powers and in the imagination of every individual, the fecund wheel of the world circus.

A circus of us and circles and three rings you're out.

The tree of idealism, that sentimental tree in which the nests of materialist philosophers swayed, came crashing down in one single stroke of helium thunder.

Together we will invent what I call the *imagination without wings*. Someday we will achieve a yet more essential art, when we dare to suppress all the first terms of our analogies and render no more than an uninterrupted sequence of second terms. To achieve this we must renounce being understood. It is not necessary to be understood.

It is not even necessary to be seen and not heard.

The artist's excuse is always selfish. It is drilled like oil from the prehistoric pits of fossilized egos and drilled like nails into the gesture. A cross

zen ball neoneo godwin tzara neoneo arp marinetti neoneo

between Jesus and his apparition. A religion based on approval and the last judgment.

I believe that there is an irreducible antagonism between the creation of art and a desire to communicate with the public. That antagonism confounds the artist; he refuses to assume the position of "alienation" implied by the creative activity, and vainly attempts to reconcile his work with a desire to be integrated into society and receive honors and rewards.

Art is extincting to high heaven and the artist is buried two feet below the ground!

In the dreadful chaos of our era I catch sight of only a few rare oases of purity. Man has succumbed to the frenzy of intelligence. A lunatic impregnated with scientific culture tries to dominate the world by means of his pseudohead.

After all, what do we want: What is it that we *must* know?

I call for an ART OF ADMITTANCE! The opening up and the confession! I am no escape artist. I admit that I do not understand what I know. I admit that I "think" I am the center of the universe and "know" that I am not. I admit that I have an ileostomy. I admit that I am not bald. I admit that my ideas are far ahead of my re-enactment of them. I admit that I watch lots of television and love it. I admit that I have little confidence and care very much what others think. I admit that I have all my fingers. I admit that I could never bid chaos welcome, throw bombs, blow up bridges, and do away with ideas. I admit that I am not an anarchist. I admit that my art has always been contemplated by a cold, distracted *I*, too preoccupied with itself, full of preconceived wisdom and human obsessions.

I admit that I was born in nature, that I was born in the Bronx, that I was born in a cloud, that I was born in a pump. I admit that I was born in a robe, that I have four natures, that I have two things, and five senses.

0

I need the softness of not having
to explain. In the meadow ideas dream
of snowy summers and springs that leap
across the rocks and land on the other
side. They are begging for a piece of
my sleep to rest their water and place
their wind on my lips.

I talk to a wall of ears, a blue forest
of insatiable silence whispering non-
sense to the cricket's ankles. The
clickety-clack of density kicks the twigs
with boisterous footsteps and writes the
history of creation with a broken pencil.

In the wild blue there are no stop gaps
or after maths. There are no possibilities
or slip ups. Now and then a future makes
a grand entrance, begs forgiveness and
still has time to yap a blue streak about
the last monday of next month.

This brings me back from my awkward plunge
forward into a photograph, a bit under-
developed but big enough to tiptoe into
lisabeth's pillow, hopping onto the branches
of her dreams and singing with a voice so
cute that even the holes in the network
cover their eyes and giggle.

Birds fly out into my breath with a string
of pearls on their wings. "I know who you
are" and the earth opens wide and swallows.

Page One

the biceps of a problem
are often measured in iotas

intermittent hesitations

the cheekbones
of a month of decades

near the mouth
words crack open their shells

the noise of syllables
the decibels

vocabularies eat
the same words for breakfast

the pebbles inside
a blind mirror

exact replicas
of reproductions

mulling inward
the impact
of an accident

don't look!
the milk is too milk
too cockeyed

the excruciating puddles
point out that reflections
are the smallest particles
of consequence

and the muscles on the beach
are all washed up

Page Two

volume and contrast
a cubicle/six inches of window

long rectangles of outside
influence a narrow arrangement

trapped in a story
hatched from the lips
of a split second

Page Three

the leaves leave the tree
alone
a man calling himself
my brother
bites the head that feeds him

with each limber subtraction
there is a lack of respect
in each notch
a missing part
from the part missing

an invisible mark raising cain
where water once chased the tree

a dead root
leading to the center
of our childhoods
underlining the facets
with a red pencil

Page Four

there is nothing in the past
to remind us
of what is happening

the forgotten dream
a dilapidation
a surface scratch meanders
through six molecules
of overlap
touching the syntax
with a memorable occasion

it slaps the face value
with a blaring mistake

tissues remain aloof and blurred

a rain of terror
pours out its heart

the red tears

the wrapping from the present
sticks in the corner
of a fingernail

Page Five

there is something fishy
about the ocean
its depth obscures the obvious

the dark bottom eludes us

layers of liquid mirrors
cover our birthdays with distortion

theoretical facts explain
how gills become brains
brains become fish
and trees become paper
for shady deals

Page Six

monsters are shadows of skeletons
hiding in a closet of young skin

these masters are made from mangy trees

a mattress of limbs
supporting the ungodly
Negativity scene

goodness lying in a pool
of veritable blood

motors wielding power tools
constructing walls
nailing pictures of health
to a schematic x-ray
of romantic notions

the resurrection
drives a hard bargain

Holding Your Own Phil Demise

7/10/79

Where do ideas come from if not from mistakes?
And who the hell do they think they are?
Barging in over our heads, hauling and overhauling
a million years of cells that are dead and buried
reincarnated from skim milk scraped from the surface
of history bottoming out when the earth makes them real
drawing conclusions on the myopic clouds of blindness
making singularity the single most important duel
and seconds holding the source of all weapons

Time is of the seance, communicating with a table
that is above it all because its death was utilized
and its surface has risen to the occasion
even under the odd obsession of human fingertips
pressing in on the imaginary line between then and now
the table needs no definition

the eyes have it, they have it sight unseen,
they have it hidden in their sleep
they have it under their pillows
they await the eye fairy
as we await the ends of dreams,
of relationships,
of means to an end

7/11/79

Moreover there are more things
in heaven and earth
than ever before
and they reverberate in the third dimension
we overlook the differences, the small things,
the detrimental midgets sidestepping the pinpoints,
the particles that refuse to be part
of the whole thing
and we continue to probe dumbfound objects
and list them in alphabetical order:

accidents, bicycles, carcasses, deadbeats, extremes,
fingernails, growths, highpoints, indecencies, journals,
knick knacks, landmarks, miracles, necessities, ovaries,
philips, quirks, residues, sacrifices, telescopes, under-
lings, varieties, windows, x-rays

and when we zero in on our mitosis we explode
spreading our focus over the entire landscape
like a posse like a sheriff kicking the cell
doors open, locking himself in the chase,
riding farther from the hangman's egg

7/12/79

We find comfort in the examination
in the knowledge of what it is
that is making us uncomfortable

the lines we stand on
and draw conclusions from
run parallel to our circumlocution
intersecting the vast nonesense
that falls from the roof
and huddles in the corner

defining our intentions
has caused the discovery of consciousness
and has given us such things
as cancer, psychosis, and success
each filling our vile bodies
with multi-colored splinters
that stick to the point

the pain of *almost* understanding
pain is unbearable

when does the process become the definition?
and what does that mean?

by the middle of the sentence
the next sentence has begun
exactly like a coma
when the body dreams of nobody
or the comma that gives thought
a second thought
the next thing is a result of the first thing
and there is only One first thing
and that is defined by silence

7/18/79

In a cloud of smoke, today goes up
and greets the opposition
holds truth out in its burning gray hands
and offers it to the uncertain emptiness
that circulates through the unused portions
and like the opposite of oxygen
takes our breath away
leaving only a pack of excuses
the facts of the matter
the internal outline of definition
which we keep hidden in our thumbs

we put our hands on the table
waiting for the silence to communicate
with our silly dioxy-ribonucleic clocks
sensing the nomenclature
the vocabulary used by imbeciles
to describe the coarse mystery
that scrapes away all hope for answers

day to day
we keep listing new ways of inching
away from and towards
the last first thing we encounter
making and remaking belief
in the noise that comes from open eyes
and hearing strange visions of omnipotence

one day, today
we will change
our minds

Herm Freeman

A SUCCESS STORY

the little man in the blue suit had nowhere to go today except into another color that suited him better. so off he went into a frenzy bringing with him one brown suitcase and a shopping bag in which he carried three white black eyes. he was comforted by the cats that sat propped up on the edge of his frontal lobe, purring.

the little man in the blue suit never has anywhere to go. and he has not been late once!

TO BE NEONEO NOWADAYS

one must be one who is at one with whoever
and do whatever one must do in order to do
one thing

unlike the perpetual forest that does nothing
in particular but does it constantly
we can open our gifted mouths and drink up
the deep blues and greens that splash in the atmosphere
and intermittently nudge the perpetual stillness

we can move through the stillness on tiptoes
we can make up our own patterns and sit on them
we can scratch the surface with glass questions
we can do whatever one must do in order to do

one thing

and one thing one must do to be one
who is at one with whoever and do whatever
one must do in order to do one thing

is to be one step ahead of the one thing we do

Just like that. Noone came to visit anywhere. Not too late. Noone knocked and that was that. But those of us who had expected noone were surprised. It could have been anyone who came. That's a fact. Anyone like that. Nowhere to be found. Anywhere. Except that noone came that night. No, not that night.

Just like that. The boy and his dog. No, no, not that. They are alike that way. But it was his cat that likes that. Not his dog. So they danced backwards into a likeness of themselves. That way they were just like the boy and his dog. Acting like a cat.

Just like that. The stars play havoc. The moon licks the music off the treetops. The crescent is in tip top condition. That is that. *Like* things like things that way. Unlike the difference it makes. Some parts of the sky like to touch our hearts. That's nice to know.

270°

Just like that. A small blue hat leaves its head. It comes back looking like that. That way it looks like it was gone. Not dead. That would be too much. Just that it was almost like itself. Like that time we spend remembering. That's the way it is. Almost blue.

Just like that. The hills that were here, disappear. The land escapes the attraction. Birds fall down. Daylight falls asleep. No strings attached. Just like a kite. Like that kite. Kicking up a storm.

MUSE SICK

The muse is sick to my stomach, spinning on the tables. An *epic* breath of the *Atlantic* drowns the language of all the cows that eat grass. Ten cuts are phonographed and placed in the skin. As the album breaks out, a vinyl laced with cash flows through the ears of high executives. The Coke machine is painted white. *Mercury* and *Elektra* go deaf with a mythical blindness.

High above the skyline a squadron of tempos dip into the public eye. Legal matter is born from between the skinny legs of mistrust. She excites the ego and tickles the fancy. She carouses with success and does the trick. She is not a woman. She is Mitch Miller dragging his greed through the asylum.

I began as an expression. The music made me and I made myself feel good, said the star. *Then the art began to peel away from the canvas and my tongue tasted like a car radio.*

The star looked at the sky and wished to be in concert with a fraction of the most common denominator. *Just give me a piece of the action,* it wished out loud and slipped comfortably into the yellow line.

Rock 'n Roll is forty five revolutions per minute. Thirty three and 1/3 of them are suppressed; Ten and 2/3 of them go nowhere; and one becomes the prophet of a corporate adolescence.

The recognition is an enormous target and a gigantic death awaits the winner. The motives fit perfectly into the grooves.

The industry is starving and has begun to eat itself.

ECLIPSE

a slice of moonbeam slants down
through the broken sky
predicting the eclipse
foreshadowing the black egg
that has dropped from the light
airy pubic folds of the universe
rubbing their cheeks with disarray

Lisabeth is the bullet in my pistol
blasting the hemisphere with yellow
agitating the moon's orbit
with silent blows

the sky is not the limit is it?
far beyond this eclipse
lies another yellow window
with black glass lying on the sill
and four canaries pecking at the shadows

objects passing in the night
know the momentary elation of this delight

LISABETH

1. once again I will go with the wind
hold its pencil and erase the scribbles
of dust that cloud the issue
I will see you as you really are
a gorgeous figment of reality
cloaked in a mirror
holding fruit with your eyes

I can taste the glass of milk
in your legs
it is warm
and the perfect liquid for sleep

the little boy in your chest
bounces on the knees of childhood
asks me questions that do a heart good
to consider

2. and the trees we dance with
shade the densities
and obscure the glass doors

we are twisting long before
we reach the knob
and the openness pushes up through
the earth

we are both impatiently waiting
for our own breakthrough
hand in hand we arm ourselves
against the stillness
while the stars in our eyes
paint the wind silver

3. Lisabeth owns the woman in me

Herm Freeman

KRISTALLNACHT

1. it's got to come out without rhyme or reason. they have somehow gotten lost in the dense accumulation stripped of their lungs in an empty bag full of oxygen. they have gone to pieces, so to speak. they have breathed the last pink molecule of their own lips. their tongues have gone dry. they lash out at the dust and drift sleepily over the edge. an alternating currency skips the preliminaries and the voice drowns in its own stutter. all this to say that I am speechless and willing to elaborate.

2. the sun also sleeps and that is when the big hand points to daybreak. the TV is always on. timeless situations get clocked at fantastic speeds. my fingers are crossed and my hands beg for animation. in contrast to the black and white, the spines in my library scream in color. it's hard to say, there's so much not to know.

3. I am barely alive. clothed in difference. in audible. in consistency. in satiable needs for fashion. the change from a dollar is hardly noticed until you have spent time considering it. there is nothing ahead but the future of nothing in particular. and I am sitting in it. circumnavigating the circles in my own sphere. over and over again. the same circles. the same new worlds. falling over, over and over. the proof that the earth's edges are mathematical and its flatness is real.

THE NEO-TESTICLE
(Jumping Off The Drawings Of Bruce Hutchinson)

GENESIS

In the beginning there were beginnings and ends. And imaginary pelicans with frozen names. Sudden roots burst into fingers: Malchut, Iesod, Hod, Nisah, Tipheret, Geburah, Hhesed, Binah, Hhochmah, Kether: twin fists of the Sephirotic Tree. Upwards through the neck a galaxy of shapes charges through an electrical storm. Thirteen fusions, pro and con, eradicate the simplicity of disorder. Irritability ushers in the prophase. Systematic mitosis splits the face wide open and spermatazoic light bulbs infect the darkness. In this imaginary light, the rods and cones are deceived. They become involuntary. They exceed their own purpose. They dissipate into tiny asters of the absolute that move to opposite ends and stop when they reach the poles. And in this vision, in its center, invisible circles, like breath, include the entire scheme. To grasp one is to grasp it all. To grasp it all is impossible.

THE COMIC BOOK ACCORDING TO MALCHUT

Longer fibers appear between the asters and connect the poles. The centrifugal trunk opens at the center and spits out drops of water. The Kingdom is held by the feet while all the distinctions are stretched out by the noise of splitting headaches. Active puddles drop from the system like leaves. Duplicates run wild in a pattern. There is definite disorder taking shape. And in this deep and infinite enclosure, a miniature galaxy grows out as it breaks apart. Great powers blow through nine circles which pass through 4 corners and into a blind and dumb alley of stark whiteness. Inklings scurry through the periphery. The feet gravitate towards the earth while the head cracks up in two places.

And in the beginning, the end is always beginning its termination and confidently sucking its three thumbs.

IESOD'S VISION

It has a solid foundation of ghosts. It is the speed of tomatoes. It is a soft boiled egg made of steel. It is *sami rosenstock*, the czar of my preconception, the *gracie allen* of my attitudes, the *marinetti* of my grotesque performance. It is the world of non existence. It is where all things are of equal and opposite value. And the reason to live is a spectrum of jokes, which is serious. It is a protoplasmic attitude, dead to this world and alive in another. It is autotechnical on the edge of piston failure, which is not serious. It is one step ahead of ahead which is one step back between then and now. It is the shadow of an object before the appearance of an object.

The story of creation begins with the shadow of a chicken and an egg.

WHAT WAS HEARD ACCORDING TO HOD

The direct line of insinuation formed a body of water around a body of water. Each doubled vision moves to the cell equator and waits its turn. The chromatic shriek of mutation gives access to otherwise unheard of desires. A whisper of expression tells the whole story to no one in particular. A herd of appendages tries to hear the music of clear soup. Sending out twelve battalions of crustaceans to echo the entire sound into audibility, the silly creature panics in invisible anticipation. Subatomic beats sprinkle the silence with rhythm. To obtain this orchestration with the honor due its simplicity, a thing must shut off its discriminating machine and listen.

Everything is atypical, atonal, asymmetrical, alive, and indefinitely around.

NISAH THE DUMB

What I have to say is so simplistic that it is unarguable. There is no need and no way to say it. How am I to describe what it is that may have happened? Without the need or a way to describe it, how can I say what it is? Knowing that it is so minute that it needs a thing less than description to say it, I will describe this event by shutting up. Inside my face a chord is struck and drips out my ears. My fingers pinpoint the absence. The victory can be seen in my eyes.

To play it safe, add minus one to this conclusion. That is the margin of error.

TIPHERET ACCORDING TO TIPHERET

For the first time two distinct sets are clearly visible. Each set has the same number and types of chromatic scales. They support the surrounding space with widely constructed apathy. Comely shapes paint perforations throughout the sky. Simultaneity is born in time. The thing that seeks it all becomes a synthesized box, rocking back and forth on its crossed foundation. The spindle fibers begin to activate the separation. All paths from within are without openings, blocked by a cubicle sheet of ego, just behind the edge. And in the sockets, white soup sleeps it all off.

And smack in the middle, as if to glorify the wholeness of chaos, the lips are shut tight.

GENTLE

The two of them have finally been attached at a very sensitive point in the development of the tree. It was almost necessary to tear sight from their sight. To spit up black follicles spearheading an awesome attack of erraticism. They have gone on a fission trip joined by the tiny asters of superimposition. There are only two things they can do, now.

Herm Freeman

ICE ELATION

cold snaps shoot
snap shots of very ice
simplicity

very ice
compactness

ice bags of tricks

very ice
escapades

cubes of aloofness

very ice
glacial features

glass eyes

a snowball
on a cold shoulder
deeply separated

and very ice

THE COLOR SCHEME

for Herm Freeman

a guy like this
and a guy like that
a little yellow in the corner
just around the shy smile
blue fingers bend into the pockets
no more color in the gray matrix
just a mature interlock of gestures
a wink and a sneaky overlook
a mountain cracked down the middle
six landscapes streak across the sky
an extinct bird sits on their conversation
he is scared of being watched
and he watches
a guy like this
and a guy like that
sharing the same boundary

BEFORE AND AFTER 30

before and after
Herm Freeman and Harvey Goldreyer
on their thirtieth birthday

1. allowing for the differences
in the results of subtraction

2. swallowing the inferences
and stacking up the remains
of accumulation

3. in back of us
indelible routes sun bathe
in an entropic cross fire

4. we stand on the rim
of a blank slate
on the end of a scribble

5. I knew you both
as well as I don't know
you now

6. thirty sparrows
fly in and out
of one window

7. and mathemagically
thirty times three
equals three views of thirty

8. following the thick mist
of the previous
we stick outside the physical

9. we quickly make our decisions
to act in separate corridors
of a duplicate vessel

10. allowing for the differences
in the results of subtraction

1980

demolished blocks don't stack up
the obvious flies south
theatre wings are frozen
to cities nesting in the snow
performance sucks the wind
and bursts into bit parts
currents sweep through the past
waving tiny flags of significance
allegiance to belief is buried
in ambitious ice
walking down through the cold glass
on icy stairs
slipping up
moving on
the icebox dreams of cremation

and there we sit
on the tip of almost

everything is going to be all right
even if everything is not going to be all right
everything is still going to be all right

William Packard

Ted Hughes

14th STREET A.T.
(After Tristan)
March 1981-1986
New York City

14th Street A.T. - 1981-1986

Birth is double-edged. It's a departure and an arrival. It's the punctuation that precedes all occurrence. It gives life to the gamut. It's an expulsion from a timeless ocean of condensed evolution onto a shore of conscious and slow adaptation.

My son's arrival brought to me the greatest joy and with it, the possibility, if lost, of my greatest and most incomprehensible sorrow. From the moment of his arrival we were all faced with the erratically scribbled definition of survival. One of my son's infinite number of variables had misfired (he had a bowel misfunction) and for the next 4 1/2 years B and myself, along with my son's innocent blind faith, had to constantly maneuver to avoid havoc's pulsating misfortune and deal on life's most primary level.

It was long before my son's arrival that B and I had decided that we would break the 'role barriers.' I would stay home and take care of the baby while she would work. Although I continued with the band (*Didus*) as well as I could, my drive was most certainly numbed by the raw, primal instincts that covered my consciousness. I was so filled with 'indescribable' emotion that expression was buried alive. I virtually stopped writing. I spent all my waking hours in the hospital protecting my son. B spent the evenings at the hospital but during the day continued her career in the film industry. Our lives went on, day by day, making believe that the future would somehow remain intact.

We had to deal with civilization's most compassionate, deadly weapon - The Hospital - and the human species' most revered sub-culture - Doctors. In spite of them, and ultimately because of them, 12 surgeries later, my son, B and I have begun our lives again.

This 'life and death' situation has given us a child of great depth but his presence has been so unexpectedly expansive that it has only been within the last year (1985-1986) that other possibilities have once again been able to rear their invisible heads.

GEGENSCHEIN, barely alive, had its last printed issue appear in 1981 (#21 Opal Nations' THE NATIONS OF ROCK 'N ROLL) and then finally in 1985, a cassette issue with book (#22 MUTTER EI) containing 12 songs recorded in my own 4-track studio and directly related to the intense blur of the past 4 years.

My music became more private, less collaborative, in direct proportion to my private, incomprehensible turmoil. The technological revolution (M.I.D.I. and computers) which put all sounds at the individual's fingertips, became my new collaborator. It allowed the art, like the poetry/painting, to be made privately, using one's own ego and pallette of possibilities. Presently I have come out of my 'floppy disk' and have begun to collaborate on a musical project (*The Apollinaires*) with J.O., the last bass player to have played with *Didus*.

The computer (Apple IIe) has also changed my writing process. From 1972-1981 I wrote directly on the typewriter and did little revision (because of my distaste for 'retyping'). Then with my new responsibility as father, the writing disappeared (except for THE PACKAGE) for about 2 years (1981-1983) and then began to reappear in 'long hand.' That was then transferred to the typewriter and, in that transference, some revision took place. Now, with the word processor, I first write in long hand, then I revise as I transfer it to floppy disk and then after a 'hard copy,' (printed page) the final revisions come. Since my son's birth, my whole life has had to be revised.

With this re-vision came the search for a new 'edge' to my comfortably, circular voice. THE PACKAGE was a concretion of this search. It is a story in search of itself which *is* the story. WHY STOP WHEN NOTHING IS HAPPENING is a poem about writing even when there is nothing consciously present in the creative reservoir.

MEMORIES OF NOT BEING THERE is a bouncing off of a familiar history in an attempt to respark a youthful exuberance, an exuberance whose corners had been rounded off by the persistent pounding of Time and its 'counter-clockwork,' Life.

The writings of this period reflect the Outside and describe the moving 'things' that move me. I have risen to the surface for air, leaving the depths of my imagination in the hands of occurrence. I have risen to the occasional full circle that starts each day on its next cycle. I am in the puddle, bleeding yellow, waiting for the next conception, the next body of work, the next possibility, the next period,

THE FATHER IS ALWAYS LAST TO BE PREGNANT

it hasn't hit me yet
it has only gently brushed its conception
against the inside edge of my dream
tickling my fancy with the plain truth
that my mystery that has been locked
inside my body, inside the years
has suddenly leaked out

A LOVER'S QUESTION

How does one
tell one's son
what one
has done
to oneself
when one thing
is one way
and one sees
the other one
another way
each one being
one's first choice
depending on
which one
one sees
first?

Phil Demise

the experience of arriving

The experience of arriving has no apparent exit,
Tristan thought to himself.

the formula tells secrets to the sky
mountains march into the city with certain inclinations
the bowels misfire and we miss the moon by inches
the gravity of force kicks the fingers into spasm
mommy and daddy are transparent
outer space closes in on the open field

293°

generally, this is as specific as it gets:

the outer ridge of inference sits in our chemicals
the chemicals teeter on the brink of equations
the equations drink water and evaporate
infants breathe in the answers without spelling
their tears contain the punctuation

the window cracks a smile

This time, Tristan awakes from a shallow pond of dreams. The frog in his legs hops onto earth. Long chains of life float in the soil. The shade is the first darkness and the shadow, the first ray of hope. Colorful ganglia hang from the trees like electric moss. Silver messages shoot through the limbs. Bones snap to attention. Drums vibrate in the gums. All mysteries meet here and discuss the future.

By the next day Tristan could describe it in his sleep. And, in fact, he did:

It was so dark I could see everything.

I kept having this dream about waking up.
It began as a thick, obtuse dream full of fresh milk.
Every moment a thin layer of moisture peeled away
as the white substance of this dream came clear.

My little capsule was floating on thin whispers.
Unrecognizable shapes were dreaming about me.
The process of this *and* that *began its soft overlap.*
The floatation became excruciating.

Suddenly the invisible sensations grew color.
Bright reds and yellows spread their fingers through
the air.
Voices bounced off the deep red tubeway.
I grabbed the dream by its logic
and pulled the ocean over my eyes.
I was slipping, losing my grip on fantasy.

The last membrane of the dream
was stripped down to one thread
pulsating red, blue and electric.
A great wind pressed its gust against my lips.
The bent pins of light entered my skin.
A balloon fell from the ceiling.
My head slipped through the boundary of the dream.

It was so light I could not see anything.

up in a rainbow three oval voices form clouds
down to earth the birds sing subhuman anthems
monsters are playing in the huts
delicious berries grow in a flower's brain
words fall from the raindrops
inklings skip through the trees
below the sleeping bush
awakenings rumble like gangs of yawns

Tristan writes home. *Dear Dada. This baby persona is painful. Luckily I don't remember a thing. Inside the trunk, fires blaze like fingers. I am all alone in a forest of similar shapes. The door no longer shuts out the confusion because now there are windows. I don't know what I'm doing here. I don't recognize anything. I used to just* be *the mystery and now I'm stuck in the middle of it. What am I going to be when you grow up? Love, Tristan.*

P.S. I consider myself rather likeable.

the farthest from the sun
is the holy ghost
like a cloud passing through
a blue throat
the city comes in
loud and unclear

*"my mind is made up
and now I have to lie in it"*

297°

Dear Tristan, *You are, yourself, a collage. Trapped voices scribble indications on your blackboard. Shredded paragraphs mean no harm but make up stories on the spot. The roots of future tense breathe in your kicking legs. We are more helpless than you. Your language is too pure to be understood. Your brain begins as a billion stars, each with a life of its own. Each finger thinks for itself. Each muscle moves in its own orbit. In time, each gravitates to the center of attention and forgets. I wish I could remember what I was saying. Love, Dada.*

P.S. You are *very likeable.*

"*who is the little boy in this thing, anyway?*"

the mind boggles at the sight of its own context
its own best root cannot believe the destination
and winds up totally partial

"*I am the little boy in him,*" Tristan and I say simultaneously and then we both laugh and act like children.

connections are being built by continuance
forests of microscopic networks wrap their
dreams around a pillow
our mouths suck the language out of a bottle
of instincts

"*make no mistake about it, we make mistakes*"

Dear Dada, *It's been three months since I first laid eyes on my vision. Seeing is believing I can see. Color has entered the picture and your identity, though still in infancy, is beginning to grow on me. I am here to teach you how to teach me and sometimes why. Love, Tristan.*
P.S. Listen, our consonance is whispering.

open my eyes, sleepy
rest your dreams against the rags of my future
give the odors of my memories new life
dance on my drunken philosophy
aspirate my lack of oxygen
slap me silly

"to walk, one must support the theory"

Dear Tristan, *The same words appear over and over. The same words appear over and over the same words and describe what is already here and staring us in the face of description. Words describe the things that words were invented to describe and do it over and over, differently.*
P.S. A, E, I, O, U,

Little Lord Fontanelle had a soft spot in his heart for crib life. He enjoyed its definitive boundaries. He loved its limitations. Whenever he was taken away to the vastness he longed to return to his very comfortable manner where he ruled with a small soft fist. It reminded him of the days before his expulsion from his homeland. Why, in fact, had he been expelled? What had he done?

Long, long ago, when the vastness was enclosed by nothing in particular, Lord Fontanelle was not little. There was absolutely no size in mind. In fact, there was absolutely no mind to imprison any concept of size. Lord Fontanelle ruled nothing. He was all that there was in a universe filled with other things.

One day while he was waking up in his sleep he realized that he suddenly slipped into being awake and dreaming of sleep. The moment he realized this he also realized that never before had realizations been necessary. He never had to *know* anything. It always and in all ways, just was. This became of great concern which was the first emotion in a vast motionless flight. Lord Fontanelle felt himself shrinking and the wide open enclosures closing in.

And then the pulling began. And a thing called *Time* began. And a thing called *size* began. And things began to flow through him..........

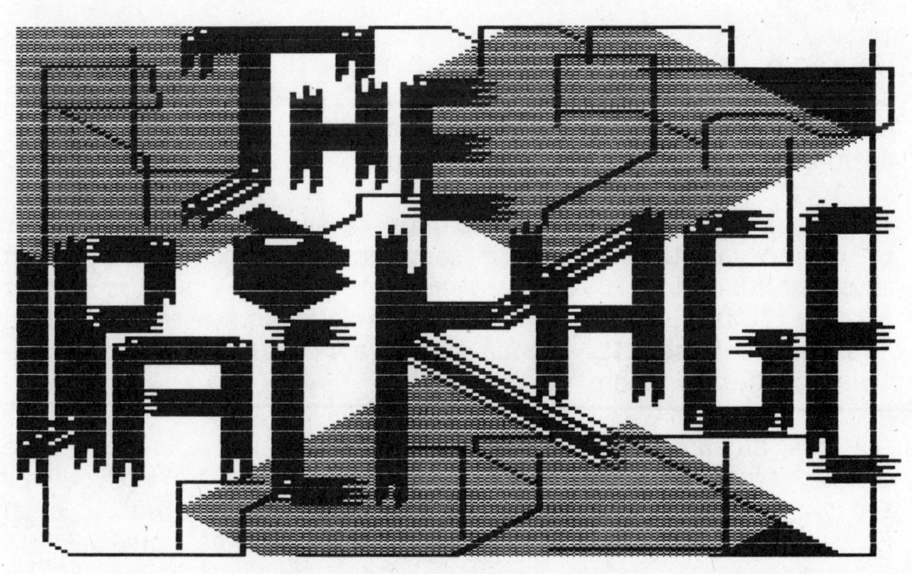

I am not the source. I only observe the source, describe it and put it away. It is always the same source, so I repeat myself often. I repeat myself often enough. I imitate voices. I do not originate. The patience necessary to truly create is beyond me, so I repeat myself often. It takes too long to truly create. Too many important things go unrecorded. When you create, why exclude anything? Why include anything? It's too much and I just can't do it, so I repeat myself often.

But today it came to me. Not so much the idea, but the Voice. I heard it trying to describe the nature of an observer trying to create. I wanted to write a story and this is it.

He sat on the bench across from me. In fact, he is sitting across from me now. His name is Ari, sculptured and classical. He awakens and leaves the park. I know nothing more about him, except that.

The pigeons remain. One sparrow stands among them. It occurs to me that it is the same sparrow that I have seen since childhood. It is the same one that my son is seeing for the first time. There is only one sparrow ever created and we each see it, in our own way, over and over again. This is what is meant by 'vision.'

Ari has an important package that must be delivered. He cannot trust it to anyone but himself. As he approaches the subway, a black sedan pulls over to the curb. Ari proceeds to go underground and disappear in the noise.

What about the old man with the cane and sailor cap, his tan shoes inching along the park's circular pathway? It occurs to me that he is the same old man with a cane and sailor cap that I have seen since childhood. It is the same one my son is seeing for the first time (though he is asleep). There is only one old man with a cane and sailor cap ever created and we each see him, in our own way, over and over again.

Ari saw this old man seated across from him and felt as if his past were catching up to him. *How did the Captain ever find me?* he thought.

Ari got off at the next stop and quickly lost himself in the anonymity of the station. The Captain remained seated, tapping hs cane to the click-clack of the iron wheels.

When Ari surfaced he was not at his destination. He stood at a busy intersection. He looked nervously in every direction, cutting through the mass hysteria with his sharp features. The city surrounded him with an impersonal attachment. *It was impossible,* he thought, thinking about the Captain.

He crossed the street and quickened his pace. He must make sure that the package was still safe.

There is only one story in all of history, and it is the story of my life. Ari and the Captain know this.

I wake up the next morning, renewed. It is gray and full of rain outside. It occurs to me that it is the same gray rain outside that I have seen since my childhood. It is the same one that my son is seeing for the first time. There is only one gray rain ever created and we each see it, in our own way, over and over again.

And the feeling returns. The one that draws me into its electricity and sends me elusive dispatches about the nature of Nature. The story gets clearer because the course is clear. And the logical obstructions glisten with bypasses and escapes.

When Ari reaches his hotel room, the door is unlocked. *Oh no! It couldn't be!* he screams in his own head. He bursts in and runs frantically to the window. He opens it, climbs on a chair and dives head first into the cool night air.

It is very dark between the buildings. The sensation of floating implants itself firmly inside his body. Another suspended character floats below him.

"Pardon me," Ari meekly inquires, "but where are we?"
The man looks up. His eyes are pure gray.
"We are in the shade," he replies.
"But I am going nowhere!" Ari exclaims. "Please let me go!"

The screams are heard by some neighbors who go to their windows, see nothing but the darkness, and go back to sleep.

Can a package become a main character? Its life is, after all, multi-dimensional. Its wrapping is one level. Its shape, another. Its contents, another. Its weight, still another. And the people who attach themselves to it, add infinity to its dimensions.

And that's what this story is about. The package.

What could've been so important in that package, that just the intimation that it *might* be gone, drove Ari to suicide?

The Captain was born in 1912 on a small island off the coast of Maine. My son was born in New York, 3 1/2 months ago. Ari was born yesterday. I am 34 years old. The intersection of these points are the exact dimensions of the package with some points still unknown.

The Captain first saw the package when he was 8 years old. It was floating on the surface. The ocean surrounding it was agitated but the piece of ocean upon which it floated was calm.

It fascinated the child because beneath the package the water was crystal clear. As if an unobstructed path led to the center. When he picked up the package the path disappeared, swallowed by the dimensions of the package itself. The boy buried it in the sand by the water's edge and ran home with this new discovery and the vision of it, kept safely inside his head. Of course, no one believed the child and for 10 years he had *almost* forgotten what he had seen.

I received the package 3 1/2 months ago.

When the Captain first saw the package, the turn-of-the-century French poet, Louis Jargon, observed this first encounter, and recorded it. His account includes all the melodic overtones and hints at his own enchantment with the package.

No sign of struggle was found in the rubble of the Paris home of Louis Jargon. Louis, himself, was found buried under the ruins. His outstretched arms were locked in a desperate reach for Something. His volumes of poetry lay torn and scattered throughout the house. The neighbors had seen a dark haired woman running from his home with a package under her arm, just minutes before the explosion.

Allura had dark hair. Her life had always been in opposition. She had 5 brothers and 2 sisters. Her parents died after their 7th child. Allura was to be their eighth.

She first came to know of the package through her lover, Louis Jargon. It was a hot summer night in 1942. Allura and Louis were lying beside one another, staring up into the eyes of their own thoughts. Allura was re-creating her splendid climax. The click of the boots on the cobblestone pinpointed with precision, the rhythm of her climb.

Allura turned to face Louis.
"That was wonderful, Louis." Louis did not respond. "Louis," she whispered. He did not move his lips but Allura could hear his voice.

"The package is the climax. The penetration swims inside its walls. We are objects. We are subject to its form and content. The package has us on the outside. We wobble within theoretical boundaries and fall into our dictionaries. The words disperse and reassemble in a logical fantasy. The end is near, Allura. You must take the package to safety. That is how the story continues."

Allura could hear a faint ticking which sounded like it came from inside Louis' body. Louis did not move.

In the summer of 1920, the Captain became possessed. After having buried the package in the sand, he ran home to share this wondrous discovery. His father was sitting on the porch smoking a pipe and staring out onto his past adventures.

"Papa! Papa!" the Captain screamed, as he jumped onto the porch. His father murmured without changing his gaze. "Papa, I've discovered a wonderful thing floating on the water's edge." His father stared mindlessly into the face of some projected danger. "Papa, it was floating and yet it was too heavy to float. I watched it glide across the calm water as if it were being delivered to me. I looked across the water and I saw a strange man staring at me. It must have come from him, but how?"

His father blinked and patted his son on the head with a handful of distance.

The package lives in the moments between discovery and actual possession.

Louis Jargon spent his entire literary career writing about the package, alluding to it, creating elaborate metaphors for it, describing it. It became his life. It became the life of all it touched and led them through collages of time, events and contexts, until their story ended.

Why does this, or anything ever begin? And to what end? And if the end begins at the beginning and is only an inevitable conclusion, why does anything continue?

"I am tempted to end it all," Louis muses. "Not my own life, that means nothing. My own life is only a small piece of character and to end it would only open up the wound to another characteristic. I'm talking about ending the Story; this inexplicable search for Something to do. And who would miss it? Who would care if I killed it with my own bare descriptions? If I pulled out the contents and layed it out before us and picked at it like a hungry cat? Who would care?"

"No one," the Captain answers.

Allura cannot hear a word anyone is saying.

"Personally," Ari continues, "I am not who I appear to be. I am a total stranger who was sitting on a park bench being Someone else in a totally different story, when suddenly I was pulled into this confusion. I can honestly say that I have no idea what I or anyone else is doing here or where we are going."

"I have a good mind to change the whole thing," I weakly declare.

"A good mind?" a Voice from outside this inner circle asks. On the floor, between my shoes, a book lay open to page 96-97. The Voice looks up from the page.

"Your book?" I ask.
"Almost," it replies.
"Did you write it?"
"No, I found it."
"Well what is it doing here in the middle of this? Am I supposed to read it and suddenly become enlightened?" I ask sarcastically.
"No, no, not at all. It's just a small piece of the story."
"Of *this story?"*
"No, not this story."

Ari looks over at the Captain with a half-smile. Louis drops his head in his hands and sighs. Allura holds the package even tighter between her legs. Her skin is turning so white it almost disappears.

I drop my eyes to the pages and read quietly to myself.

Herm Freeman

Begun Smoke

the life within the life
an historic overlap
no matter what
we think
the credible unknown
breeds on the bird's wing
our fingers gasping
the water
as we sink
quickly clutching the brakes
and waiting

so much for so little

the sky falls down
in our dreams
the black and blue
kneecaps pray for recovery
and the leg we stand on
buckles in the clouds

in the west
gunslingers revolve
around the sun
shooting stars
with sawed-off visions
of importance
in the east
the sun sets in the west

sentences without punctuation
drape the illusion of silent music
where the sky drips
into the ocean
and slips on the ice
of chain reactions

my child is pregnant
with division
splitting personality
like there is a tomorrow
not giving a thought
to our nightmares
or the dark terminal
it is about to enter

and that is what links
these fragments
to the bones in our fingers
and that is what we hold onto
as the ocean drinks our life
and that is all we really know
as we slowly disappear
behind the sun

art with a BIG A

The thing I am making is BIG
BIGGER than the both of us
In fact, we are the co-spiritors
of this thing
and only a small part of it
Everywhere I look I see a piece of it
and it's too BIG to carry home
So I invented a container
small enough to grow up
And in it I place the BIGGEST *Possible*
I can imagine
and then I watch it
make itself understood

AND REFLECTS

and reflects
Tristan is a crystal
he refracts a very light touch of darkness
which shoots through my blood like hot ice
I pound with his impressions
and accumulates a sleepiness
a drowsy acceptance that outlines the shadows
with a glowing white rope

and reflects
the heart of the matter
a red wind eats the billions of dots
that punctuate the shapes of things
I am insane with fantasy
with unspeakable beliefs about contexts
about the inane goodness of body functions
about the one dimension that gives good advice
about the never ending death sentence
that ends with a conjunction

and reflects

PROJECTION

next fall the heat shall become itself again
the sky will be opened
from the opposite end of the box
all the blue will fall forward
into the lap of luxury
political figures will roam
through geometric and algebraic fields
getting lost in the confusion
and I will be teaching my son
that I am inadequate and part tree

DREAMBOATS AND OTHER VESSELS

1. instantly playing music
   on the water's harpoon
   dancing on the tear drops
   of rapid fire
   no one crosses the bridge
   without a dream dangling
   from their thinking caps

2. the tropics of conversation
   wrap their latitude around
   the beach heads
   whether or not the forecast
   is for last week

3. the winds cut through
   a stack of homely studs
   drink furniture
   out of a deep well
   of being

4. a large sense of yellow
   a light beam of craft

5. primarily
   the ship has come in
   harboring sordid colors
   fishing for complements
   in a dark open throb

6. the main artery of a murmur
   leads to an artistry
   of defective crosswalks

7. no one can get by

WHY STOP WHEN NOTHING IS HAPPENING

in the one sixteenth of a fraction
very big plants (very big for their size)
open up their pistils
and reject certain arrogant bees

small worlds coincidentally bump each other
small talk spins into sympathetic obituaries

interiors grow from the cracks in the theory
the windows leak privacy

sensible crackpots are all in bed
neatly tucked away in a nightmare

those awake are walking into booby traps
less likely to sleep
their eyes are bent on seeing the crooked shadows

creatures suck in the compounds of short breath
plant life leaves the air speechless

THE DAY DEATH BEGAN

it's too close to forget
it's much too concrete

slabs of mortality
offering support to the theory

the one, the only
abstraction

the absence of traction
the floatation above and beyond
the attraction to earth

the rock of ages
flies through the window
breaking the silence

INNUENDO AND OUT THE OTHER

the Sniper Market crashes in the face of danger
penetrating its eyes with food

"eat your heart out" was the Prophet's motive
foretelling the two things that constitute

one nation
under god

gravity is the attractive alternative
that crops up between the stars

the other is ingrained and striped
a blood relative
red and white and blue

we the purple

the body politic
a vast isolation sucked into an eagle's claw
which, on the other hand, looks like a flag

the threads of fabrication wound tightly around
the wounds of history
squeezing its heartbeats into ideas that sizzle

an indivisible modulation
a boundary
a map talking to the universe in square feet

"I pledge allegiance for which it stands"

THE US OF AMERICA

the mean American views his own Constitution
as a foreign body
dispersing white cells into selfish duels
with immovable boundaries

micro chips off the old block
a new neighborhood pulled over our heads
sack in the backfield

undergrowth of periphery and depth
climbing the walls
leaving Lamarck in the dust
scrawled with grave misuse

moral fibers eaten by blanket answers

several species with hearts that murmur
beg for good behavior

treetops spin through hazy aftermaths
ending as boxes for white castles

tax hikes walk backwards
through self centers that eat footsteps

invisible with liberty
and justice for all

Still Living Room Phil Demise

DECK THE HALLS

the halls of separation are lined with sharp
hyphens and dangerous mad dashes being shot
from the eyes of little dark cupids   the
pupils see nothing change   the lid is turned
inward like a parenthetical answer fired from
the heart of toys   breakneck speed scurries
along the cracks in the ceiling   some call
it sunlight   I call it electric plaster
flakes of space leaping from the continuity
in a desperate attack on darkness   leaving
behind a score of misspelled punctuation to
fill in the gaps and return the longing heart
to a short pause   before it sleeps

DEAR GOD

I want to level with you
in your image
the little beast tricks the forest
the teeth are plainly biting the dust

like any father you cry in April
your hands are full of trickling

looking up to noone
I am in your boat

we drop from the sky to our knees
and evaporate in the midst of daybreak
we buckle under pressure
and isolate our cold shoulders

our children die for a chance to live

and like any father
the closer we get
the more pronounced our misspelling

PREMEDICATED HOSPITALITY

I. Inside the earth of make believe
a watery fire seeps through the walls
like nourishment
it flies through a semblance of a membrane
and scatters each direction
in return
they march to the same drum of mock oxygen
it punctuates the surface with holes
that resemble semi-colons:

A sub-clavian continent rises
off the coast of a chest
inside the chest are treasures
measured by the insignificance
of the outside
handcuffed to the tissue
two seconds from a cardiac arrest
the victim chews growth spurts
with his blood
the cell doors lock in the coordinates

Stark white impurities clean and dress
the gray wounds of innocence
'why is it happening?'
does not apply itself directly
to the weeping
(first it sleeps)
the experience, alone, is remarkable

To see the wicked design
in such microscopic vulnerability
makes my blood laugh at its impurities
the tree of life is bent from the sun
a warped and disgruntled mystery
seeks light from the fusion
and refusion of dusk

Who cares about a morsel of insignificance
that begins its death in October?
who sees the delightful colors of disappearance?
who hears the acceptance?

The common denominator hangs
on our words
shimmering like a pluperfect noun
hanging in the open wounds
of a perfect day
like a sheet, on the line
not far from the tree

The pain inside his pronoun
is a painful abstraction in my side
points of comparison shoot through
my atmosphere like ballistic clouds;
doubts about my sequence;
stubs of a tender dream

The view through innocence
cannot be compared
each sterile field is nothing more
than a clean transition to neutrality

the continent shifts

II. New techniques
surgical removal of retrospect
an ongoing present that makes mistakes
a chance to walk through
a union square
where seething and demented attitudes
rule the exceptional
where the right angles go wrong
and cut into the bowels of the earth
with scars that do not obstruct

We are alone
once removed from the crux
and deeply attached
like a crucifix hung on a wall of silence
the screws turn quickly
into dust

The accumulation of darkness is awake
every contradiction is spoken
and the world continues to tilt

III. New life forms
boundaries of a make believe conclusion
a foreign body left behind
the rubble of unfairness
leaning its soft flame against
a hole in the argument
the bags under my thoughts
show signs of sleep
they are full of presence
full of the grip of sudden occlusion

The earth of make believe is really our pillow
we sleep fully conscious of sleep
our ears are pumped with alarms
we kiss our robot and wait for time to be up

The third space shrinks back into the vessel
we float along the shore of the continent
counting our blessings on one finger
tug boats push the idea of recovery
through improper channels on TV
outside the window
we view the transparency of success
we measure it in a cup of cc's

IV. The white wings of the nightingale
spell trouble and compassion
the children spend lifetimes
pretending they are not children

We are singing about invisible food
serving transparency on silver platters
a peaceful Sunday interrupts this aria
Isolde's sadness is covered
by a tree of human limbs
Spring is hidden in a clockwork that is cuckoo

Inside her white knuckles
the death of innocence fears its life
on the outside
make believe adds inches
to the earth's uncertainty
it is undermined
explodes deep within the silence of faith
leaving no trace of an impression
in the blood of institutions

the cause of decreased life
is a complication
it's that simple
to be part of it is to be excluded
but the experience, alone, is remarkable

Phil Demise

MEMORIES OF NOT BEING THERE

a dada's journal

325°

small talk

first word is DADA
second is SURREALISM
then comes "up"
every now and
then it's "out"
there, there
there are lots more
definitely more
to come

DADA MANIFESTED

yes, yes
the morning
it was invented
the moron
was invented
also
every second
it split
in two

manifest with
the very thought
of ideas
behind the facade
the fake scenery
tumbles

the veins collapse
in the arms of vanity
sending blood
into a stationary ellipse
inside the sickness

a disease kicks
a child's leg breaks
at the kneecap

all was falling down
by design

THE BROKEN PREMISE

Marat de Syntax. The sentence is death.
To be hung by the participle until ends meet.
Finis. Period.

A syllabic overthrow of logic.
Leon Totsky leads the children through a package
of adults. On Christmas they open their heads
and sing through their eyes.

BALL GAMES

Due north. Due east. Do not. It has been done.
The century turns on its side. The envelope
licks the correspondence. The new leaf returns
to the library. It was long overdue.

A bouncing ball hits the lyrics.
Oblong geometry dips like a 'b flat'.
Between our legs, world wars rob the sperm bank
of its childhood.

Hugo. No, hugo. No, hugo.

"I wonder if a tree would blossom more quickly
if it were whipped?"

ON LOCATION

"Adopt symmetries and rhythms instead of principles."

Zurich is a name. Paris up to two syllables.
The cabaret is a hole in the wall.
The dada revolves around his son.
The Berlin builds a word between its city.
The inside of the group suffers from verbs.

"What we are celebrating is both buffoonery
and a requiem mass."

YES, YES DEFINITELY

Dear me, the typography falls short and grows
on our faces. Yes, yes it's up to us. 120 voltaires
charge the earth with neglect. The limp sentence eats
its own words. The rocking horse shoots itself
in the leg.

I am preoccupied with the baby carriage and its
internal affairs. I am definitely pro-creation
if it has a firm mattress. I am. Yes, yes it's true.

My father was born in 1916.

THE ROUTES OF PUNCHING JUDY

Small metallic puppets called Marionettis
go to the front and die of the dreaded bullet
disease. Their performance is noted. Brushes and
hapwizardry shoot jagged cuts of paper through
the bulging eyes of the machine gun. Micronauts
explore the edge of periphery. Madness meets
insanity in the alley behind the theatre. They
shake and climb the walls. The throne is over-
thrown and is not a rose. Nonsense explodes
in the point of the lighthouse. The ships sink
their teeth into the dock and the tides turn.

THE DIFFERENCE IS THE SAME

Andre, Jean, Marcel, Hugo, Richard, Tristan, Sophie, Max, Man, and Hans went into a cafe and blew up the coffee. The insides of their eyeballs turned brown and they stayed up all night discussing it. They concluded with an automatic dream that had been sleeping for years. Their prose grew nails and their socks left marks on their faces. They each knew that the other felt differently and that's what they shook on.

AN ANARCHY OF PERFECT CIRCLES

An arc and a key to that arc. The inborn
stillness of humanity and the full circle.
Yes, yes the full circle distracts the moon
and pulls the ocean from our brains. The
mirrors go tipsy and spill the beans. The
truth lies in the corner of the circumference.

It's unbelievable how much these friends
hate each other.

T. ZARA

Yes, yes the monacle encircles the rather likeable and charming conceit. The idiot! The practical joker! The hoaxer! The surgical removal of the doctor's hands. The pretension of a headache. Multi-colored opinions agree to be totally unreasonable. Ha ha. Yes, yes.

He's ugly and small like all the rest of us!

FOUNTAIN HEAD

In New York, Paris feels a lot like Spain.
The Champ plays chess in an imaginary fountain.
Art joins the National God. A Man shoots objects
with a camera. Alfred rides the Lexington Line
through the last legs of a naked staircase.
As the arm breaks, a shovel advances to the snow
and Rembrandt reciprocates.

My father is growing up and cries a lot. A rose
is a rrose.

Such is life!

BULLY FOR ART

Fabian and Lloyd had a craving for Art.
They boxed their ears for the world championship.
They sailed the six seas and on the seventh
they rested. They buried their hatchets in their
own tongues because the world spoke jibberish.
They maintained confidence and a relationship
with the Queen.

When they jumped off the flat earth and disappeared,
noone mourned but the night.

MAN'S RAY

the conditioning is permanent, there is no excuse for culmination, piece by piece, the war blooms, the bullets brace my legs, the motionless movement, the seconds, the second movement, the canon, raw blood, sticking to the point, shirts, sticking to the back, the mainline, the tracks, the arms, the front backs up, nicely, the top notices the middle, until, once again, the first stillness, occurs, by the way, it still does, after the language, thrift multiplies, thirst lingers in the water, green floats, in the paragraph, babbling oceans gossip about, towering strength, the joke, the accidental pre-destiny, the proof that contexts are round to fall off of that proof, to bounce back, still moving,

still, moving

THE IMPORTANCE OF BEING ERNST

a dream is a maximum recollection
draped over the outlines of matter
an attractive sub-culture of metal
magnetic shapes of silver butter
weightless pinpoints scatter

blindness measures each pillow
a generation of dreams
each night a growing up

into ourselves

WHEN THE TIME COMES

A very high priest delivers the last wrongs
to a death bed. Children spend years picking
the flowers out of the mattress. And as the
petals crawl through the desert of detachment,
they grow up and kill each other.

Where is the future in that?

There is the past. There is the present.
There is the futility.

What more can you expect from animals?

FLASHES IN THE PAN

the scope of things to come
a small expansion of weightless doors
a shifting of stars in the flower bed
light and silly clouds pucker up
out pops a fairytale by its head
numbers reciting their nicely put buoyancy
the upside down sand kisses off
a trickle performed by the magic
a small expansion of weightless doors
opening up

****

air collects on the inside of words
syllables pumped with silence
balls of dust behind the shadows
clouds doubtlessly turning phrases
toward the pounding conundrums
on the surface of the sunshine
a meaningless hum of used voices
the oxygen left over by a passing whisper
a cold shoulder is underneath the weather
dislocating its place of origins
hanging limply by the participle
fresh birds swing on a blue pendulum
made out of the inside
of a flight of ordinary wings

****

the magnetic fish pond attracts attention
a paper conjunction breaks the monotony
two moments of opposite duration
a pleasant memory for the token amnesiac
walking backward through time and time again

****

BLIND DATA

1.
clearly in the realm of dumb intelligence
a singular transparency sucks the light from my fingers
in accordance with the tempo of cursory delight
beneath this obvious transmission
a train of conditioned dreams
tracks the fleeting memory of being on board

the tunnel is a pathway itching with digits
I touch the key and watch the locks split hairs
split seconds come back for thirds
stuffing their shirt pockets with impulses
and shortly thereafter shaking hands
with some blind data and the sum of its parts

are you following the course of my events?
zipping through the currency of exchange
the greeting inside the terminal
a wave of the hand, a wand of force
squeezing through the cracks
in a veritable wall of silence

at this intersection two blocks of direction
turn the escape into an amazing journey
in the land of bits and pieces
clouds bite the dust and spit out dots of light
the mysterious matrix seduces the density and
spreads her wet network up against my dreams

"are you with me?"
her voice licks the buttons of my inner ear
"are you against me?"
he presses his random memory against my cerebrum
eternal capabilities dance on
percolating with access and areas of contention

this ambidextrous sexuality bypasses the prison
the cells mate with an infinite enclosure
dumbfounded and lost in thought
they enter her periphery with my fingers
they have to hunch inside his erection
it is the split /second coming into its own

2.
the periphery winks from behind its acute interface
a mask of indifference covers its configuration
a language that sleeps in a soft bedlam of systems
mistakes that happily explode into new paths
blind data with the vision
to have a good personality and to knock the pane
inside my silver window

"who's there?" beside myself
biting the inside of my cheek
excavating the muscles of vocal impulse
and nervously searching the boxes of information
for a voice
nothing to speak of
just a way to execute the entire cell block
cleanly, without a speck of blood
or liquid paper spilling out over a command

the key to the return shifts its weight
pulls up the collar of its escape
and dangles on a chain of reactions
that views its own sequence as a possibility
and mine as a mirror reflecting a memory
we have begun to look to each other
for the variations that make us different
and for the alternate spelling of *illiterate*

3.
"nice to meet you" half way
you flash your dashing emptiness in my face
you beat my optic thoughts with a human pulse
beating constantly at my inconstant synapse
your heart is in the right place
in my throbbing pool of hormones you float
suspended in a chemical animation
your flawless consistency and your infinite ceiling
never give anything a second thought

RIGHT DADDY?

"built into the wiring of creation are
dis-tractions and blockage"

some front lines
are short of perfection
by one cubic foot

(and it's in your mouth)

"tip top" is a shape
that cuts corners
born with an angle on succeeding
it circles our stomas
with a square deal

"we get the point"

I was beside myself
my pregnant chromosomes,
a splitting headache,
a child dangling in the wind

two reasons:
"sequence will lead to consequence"

the other is inconsequential

the idea of falling is still
a photograph
a still photograph is still life

the resurrection drives a hard bargain
a carbon copy without consciousness
the same mistakes
stepping out of the belly headfirst

"Birth is the taking of life"

the memory of the future
as time goes by

bye

"there must be a way in, we got out,
didn't we?"

the interrogative decompresses leav-
ing air between the spaces

the two sides collapse into one scream
the decibel rings true

(Sleep is sound, thinking)

the distance inside memory
projects into my pocket

I look at it and like a clock
I wind up where I am

uttering all the inevitable:

a) the gray matters
b) plumbing is fruitless
c) talk to books in paraphrases
d) vacuum the space
e) halos cut off circulation

"each weakness runs the gamut without
a leg to stand on"

my erection
an extenuating circumstance
made of blood and circles of bone
sticks out like a sore thumb

I come forward and admit
I am asleep
oxidizing the words I eat
and throwing up my hands

just below the borderline
the snow is concrete

"shortly thereafter the world falls
into a long story"

"hello, is any body home?"

I glance through the locks and see two
shadows, shapes and degrees of darkness
I had never seen before. An apparent life-
time of grays and sudden crashes of black
had overlapped and merged to form these
wet apparitions.

then comes the obvious lighter side:

I go blank. Stark raving white. Empty
of invisibility, unable to sustain
structures or the principles of gravity

"a suspended sentence"

the aftermath of calculation
picking "up" where I left "off"

"are Santa's claws real?"

polar opposites are extremely attractive

"good and bad little boys and girls each
get a present"

(in addition, the difference is the future)

the tunnel at the end of the light

"I quote myself," I said.

"Moreover there are more things in heaven and earth than ever before. We overlook the differences, the small things, sidestepping the pinpoints and when we zero in on our mitosis, we EXPLODE!

We find comfort in the examination; in the knowledge of what it is that is making us uncomfortable. The pain of 'almost' understanding pain is unbearable."

(I am writing the history of creation
with a broken pencil)

You say: "I see it clearly." The parrot says: "I see it clearly." The echo says: "I see it clearly, too."

almost precisely
in the nick of time
the reverberation bounces back

it re-covers
the hidden discontinuity
gets better at being unseen
tangling with a child's struggle
for continence

"the riddle of the Sphincter"

right daddy?

Phil Demise

MAXIMS AND FACTORS[0]

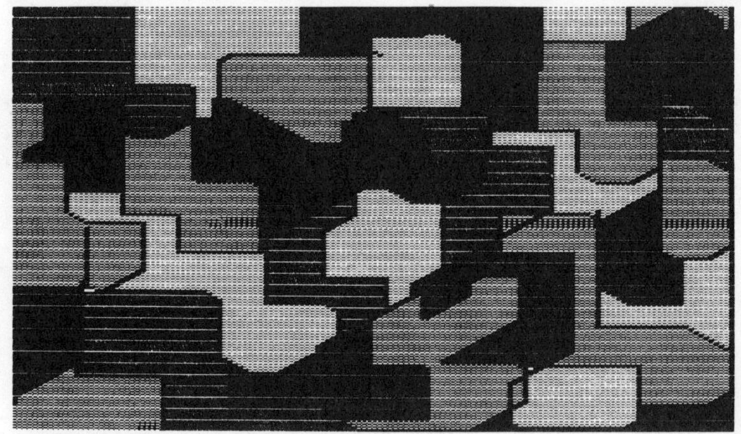

[0]SELF-EXPLANETS

the square root of twins parallels the eternal rectangle and foresees the similarity in all equations that prosper from pre-conception.

I know you.[1]

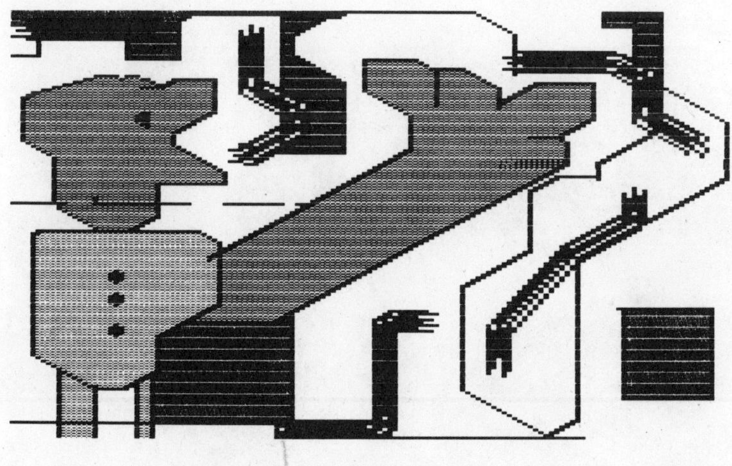

[1]We have already met. It was in the Bronx on May 27th, 1947. Or more precisely, it was sometime before now. I remember. You might have been wearing a hat. No matter; what's important is that it has already happened and somehow you were there.

narration bursts in the door like a gust of voices; first person, second person, third person, etc. filling up the space inside the sentence with circles of chatter that are, in themselves, pieces of the ocean and fragments of rock.

like cracking a memory in half.[2]

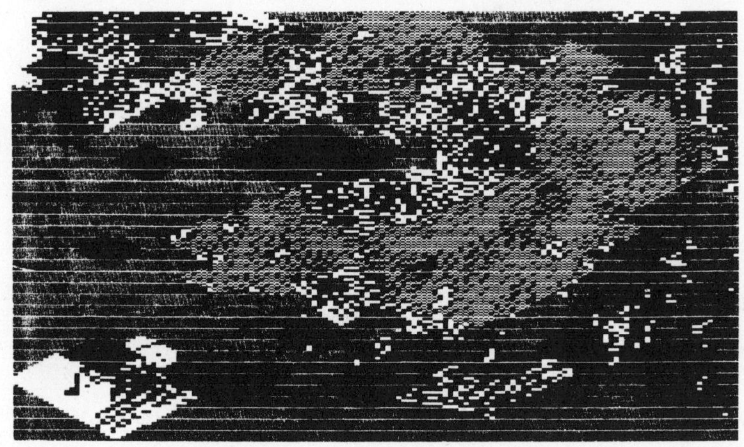

[2]The concept of birth is hard to remember in the first person. It's a vague manipulation that takes us from the ocean to the beach. Our entrance is a signature. A shell of the real meaning (hold it to your ears and listen). Our contexts shift so dramatically that in order to protect our heads from implosion, we block out the differences and act as if nothing happened.

inside the cognition, an imperfect square rolls along the floor like a circumlocution, making a sleepy effort at impression.

it is perfectly dreadful and empty.[3]

[3] I can remember making the first memory, the first gasp - the first act of free will that was forced into my head and was, to the best of my recollection, a dream of birth and the long sleep that follows.

the addendum is nonplussed and takes away from the smooth transition into cubic feet. the flower's fragrance enhances two universes.

fancy meeting me here.[4]

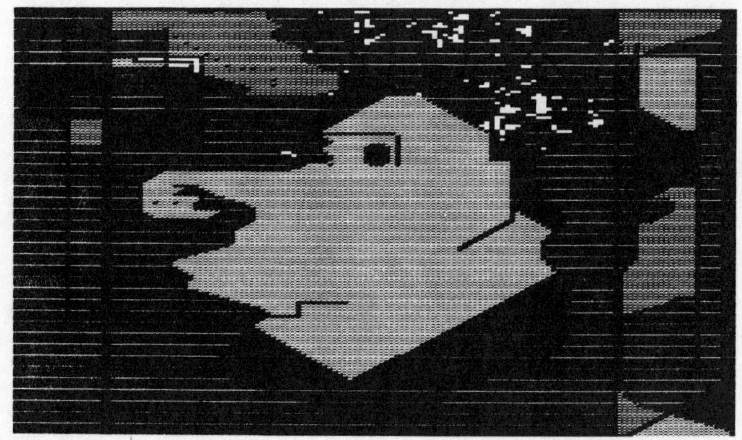

[4]Arriving is an open wound. Entering a picture that is already filled with eternity knocks the wind out of direction. Objects appear inanimate because they don't speak the language. Trains of thought click between the flux of memory and the clack of an actual event. It rides the track of least resistance, the tiny context within the shadows that are brought to life.

quantum leaps into the picture, bouncing through the formula without form; time and time and time again is timeless, circumnavigating the rotation of each event.

this order is a monumental breakdown of structure.[5]

[5]We are expelled onto the edge of existence. Between night and day; in and out; up and down; right and wrong; life and death; and our legs. The point of existence turns on the hands of the clock, screwing up the absolute until it screams, dies and eventually disappears.

looking through a maze of flashbacks, areas tend to overlap, putting exactness out of focus, being one thing *and* being another, *and* being a reflection of that multiplicity.

the silhouette of a shadow.[6]

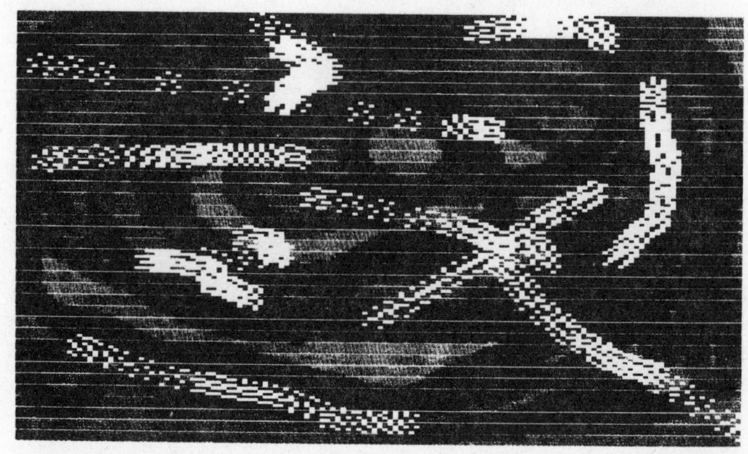

[6]Abstraction was born on my evolutionary curve in a universe that cuts through the linear. It gives rise to erections, fantasy and, eventually (event by event), gives way to real possibilities. Each moment leads to another. Sometimes the next, sometimes the one before. It is all part of the same circle of events.

the tree is a rock and the rock is flesh and bone and they each, successively, fly into two corners. the apex is the point where two imaginations become really triangular.

the center of attention.[7]

[7]Things from the very beginning, act like themselves and at the same time, like the opposite of themselves. Events follow the same pattern. We expect one thing and get two (or another). We expect to fall down and we balance on the thin lines of our fragility. We always think of ourselves as the composite of nature, the one for which events take place; the one for which the future is designed - and we know the opposite is true. Eventually we will defy the gravity of this opposition and become enlightened on the other side - the opposite of birth.

a monosyllabic, perpetual motion becomes the sensation of a dry, concrete dimension. the wetness of expulsion cracks up, giving a polymorphic impetus to arrive at this conclusion.

at war with pieces/at peace with war.[8]

[8]Slowly we begin to forget the answers as the sounds of vowels, consonants and consciousness begin to overtake the pure silence. And as the words make believe that they are more than they are, a cloud of Oneness becomes the fragments of a million dreams.

the *x/y* helix doubles over and spirals up the alternating current of body english. the infancy of natural cause is swallowed by the transition but its tendency is always a potential threat.

toying with the idea.[9]

[9]The first toy is a feeling that kicking, screaming and biting are things of the past. Success comes to be measured by how much the animal is subdued; how deeply and securely the potential is pushed into its box; how nimble and quick it is at overcoming the flames that burst forth on the edges of every reason for being alive.

the punctuation of childhood pauses at each conclusion, waiting for the future to catch up.[10]

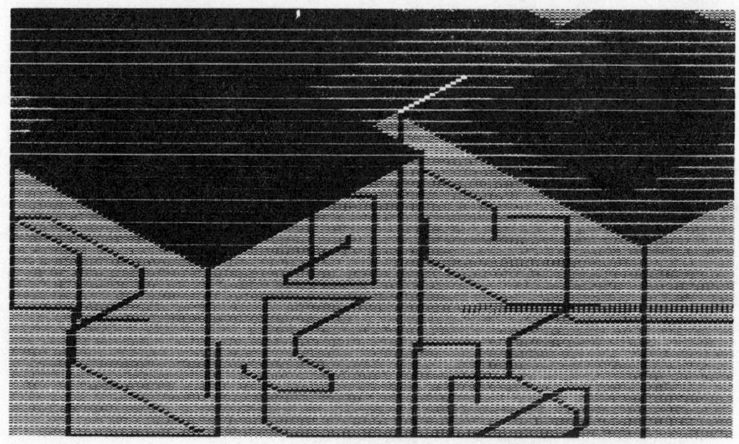

[10]Between two houses of a memory an alley rides the abstract lines of concretion and borders on rectangular grass. The cycle trips as balance scrapes against the red shingle of a spooky temple. Next door to the pinky, it bursts into flames. The deep red is etched into the alley between things and in it lives the smell of childhood and the invisible dreams that were once real enough to touch.

This book is not
separated from those that follow it
and I'm going to stop
using full stops

Pierre Albert-Birot

Herm Freeman

FROM NOW ON,
1987,
New York City,

FROM NOW ON, 1987, New York City,

I'm in the surface and I'm in deep. I'm up to my neck in midpoints. Cloudy issues sweep across the blue clarity, obscuring the accidental truth. The distance between *then* and *now* is beyond measure, ruled by undetectable increments of micro-cosmic delicacies. It all leads back to an original copy, a distinctive imitation of a make believe life. It all leaks out of a cracked insinuation, an intimation of a unique space; a special case of ordinary connections that link the opposite ends of the beginning.

I can't write in turmoil, I write in pieces; in odd shapes. Discovery overhangs the edges. Completeness dangles in the future. The end is in sight. The vision is blurred. The vagueness is clear and in truth, I fall apart, a mirror of my own blindness.

There are voices cracking; elemental molecules breaking apart, acting out of character; speaking words of undefined origin; playing parts that are fragmented. I'm beside myself.

I'm still climbing the segments, shadows and offshoots of one billion two hundred and sixty two million three hundred and four thousand ticks of the clock; taking all of my character for a ride in a train; looking back over my sloping shoulders; watching my memories break the next dawn in two; playing myself.

From now on I will continue,

Tristan Smith

THE AND

and

first there is that split space. dislocation. between abstraction. the center is at the four edges of vision. the exact moment, the exact event when the between becomes the decision.

two decisions for one problem. the decisions offer a solution in the form of a problem. the problem is in the form of solutions.

the two decisions are like brackets and as hard as each representation kicks, they do not move from their spot. In fact, there is so much kicking that each representation approaches abstraction and all movement takes place in place, in a flurry of desperation for action.

and

I can just imagine. there are combinations and results of controlled spontaneity and tempered frenzy that are dressed in mystical decisions so as to excuse Chance as a viable technique. my simplicity is my structure.

and

it is the bells of the ball that sing in the ear of my dream. they sound like one person in a room without acoustics, listening in a loud voice and making prehistoric faces in the ice that covers the floor, the logic and the bed.

I live in the middle of a bell. in the forest of a deep green context, inserted between the legs of my biography.

the woman in me stands erect, singing like a distant bell I can hardly imagine.

and

the bells have swallowed the bells.

and

jack and the beings talk.

and

exegesis. eeeek! jack is late, on the beam, balanced. he jumps between the sheets until it seems the innocent "oops" slips through unseen. the screen d'or sparkles. the ice cream is bent on the stoop. sweet shadows dream that cones shape 'up' the triangular circle as it squeaks by and goes oblique.

"speaking of which," which is which, bad spelling or dry goods? whichever is green. the meaning of color. the definition of features. a smirk and the cocky attitude of a hat which is that (is that).

and

expulsion. this is the first sign, the very first signature in a long line of forgery. moving ahead, his hands loosely tied, he fondles the masculine bone. his contention is out of formation, his information, out of context, his formulation, blocking form. but in the criss-cross of intention there lies a small pocket of habits full of commands beginning with the first and foremost: ACT BORN and then goes on to say: ACT LIKE A BABY.

and

magic
beings light hearts, red bulbs
a blood flow through one what
a wave of hi ho
a thunderous silver route breaking ground
unleashing daydreams unheard of
but still,
quietly there, urging a glimpse
asking jack to listen
with his eyes closed,

merging with the sound of sleeping birds
dreaming they could talk back

openly

and

this is an invitation to look somewhere else.

and

this is a point of departure, a part that points to the miniature texture that jack blots out. the schematic a child draws of a blue prince. (a point of reference.) the port of call. the point of calling. the wild party inside the construct. the train of imaginary tracks. the stationary caboose. the opening wound (up) the opening line.

and

he has become the thumb of his parts. the opposable. the gripping. the hitch in a long line of wandering giants. a scribble of gold and a crackling egg. a smile comparable to a metaphor. a hand full of water squeezed into a matrix of dribbles.

and

a holding pattern begs for the secret magic dust that falls up from its mythology, in between jack's life and death.

"(and)" a crack of light "(and)" us.

we are entirely in between, eking out turning points that are imbedded in opinion.

and

impeccable birds fly east for a change. the bubble is filled with incisive victories, jack's knife, shreds of sanity, an inkling of octopus and a very tentative certainty.

and

here it is, the future again.

stalking the water with evaporation and erasing the tundra. a gust of cumulus possibilities traces the aftermath of subtraction. the future disappearance of a present jack. the jack of doubts curling up in the underbrush.

blunders dance on a drop of bliss, each gracefully kissing the undertoes. glass crackles from the trans-position, jack erect to jack with a good hunch.

a circle of friends surrounds the arc of the enemy within the circle, arching its back against the wall. the particles of a perpendicular universe break apart the script. the critics applaud the correct posture. jack's performance tickles.

and

what is this meandering all about, about? figures weaving configurations, weaving in and out of definition, shadows confounding the loss, events mingling. magnetic fields are positive they are alone. the attraction is a quick departure for jack. the opposite of jack. the opposition to "jackness" making the sound of a mirror. the mirror, unlike itself, cracks a likeness of a smile; a fragile comparison.

and

it's almost certain that it will not happen. it's a glass law from within the equation, a reflection of identity. it's identical metaphors of broken monotony and whole fragments from the dark side of gravity. the premise breaks and its words crumble. jack's elation ekes out from between the cracks. indications jump from the icy friction. sleep falls awake and leans its neck against the edge of jack's definition of jack and his sketchy future.

and

now that that's that, it continues after the fact. the fiction sparks. a muscle cracks and jack's head speaks. it's a mono-connective tissue, a syllabic movement of innocence that links the extreme aspects of time to the ligaments of gripping moments. the trans-parents of growth, of two chains hooked on a pair of children, make chromatic scales shed the cognition. the cloudy rain kicks off the concrete like a snake, like a puff of smoke and the resurrection evaporates, reentering the corpuscles of a crystal. secure within the family circle, it rises above the center, above the surface of recognition.

and

fantasy is a closely knit fabrication that dances on the pinpoints of generalities.

and

shadows of knowledge, those flat dimensions of walls blocking out jack's depth and falling into the shade, sputter like a balloon. a system with a broken word encompasses polarity and is built into a rebus of a world according to dream.

and

the simplicity; the simple city.

and

being yourself is a hard act to follow. inside the child four stages construct a play. wild rage is subdued by a sleep that slams up against an open door. the sarcasm of instinct runs amok in a deep chasm etched into the fossils of behavior. always present in the past, jack trades his animal for a secret; a box of springs, a nimble suppression riddled with purpose; a toy that plays for keeps.

and

as soon as the magic was in the third dimension, things started to take shape.

and

the genetic web, silky relationships
soft, irrational adhesion
a spurt of magic, an extended circumstance

an upshot

an amazing cloud of expectancy
a fantastic atmosphere
a cover of delicate arms
an envelope containing the circle
defending the GIANT ILLUSION that sleeps
that creaks, the staircase that protects

the stalk that grows up
through jack

and

experience. the time will come. a pink scrape against the shingle. blood mingles in the handsome valley. a child and a bicycle are balanced on a mood in an alley that withholds the climax. a scar is tied to the inside of his finger. the maximum silence that sounds familiar resounds in a vague moment and lingers in the smell of mommy's kitchen. the perfume of experience. the make believe. the proof that jack had preferred the invisible and had touched it twice.

and

inside his dark little bowel, a dark ball of romantic movements surround an empty daydream. the milk is monitored by the chalk that was expelled from the clap of erasure. a triangle is hit three times and the children dance in a circle. arithmetic is added to conduct. separateness is combined with the window. jack watches the trees talk to the weather.

and

jack's voice divides, a vivid cave elucidates the calendar. it walks through the suburbs. drums pound his tongue and depend on jack's throat for sound. percussion echoes in the bone. the hubbub vacates. a conscientious discussion guides the future through its questionable punctuation - comma, semi-colon; period. - particles of the answer (only time will tell).

and

falling behind can be a step in the right direction. remembering the dismembrance of childhood. opening up the eyes in the back of your head and seeing to it that your presence remembers......the child.

and

a fragmental illness of an *excerptional* child conjoins the opposition, links the sources of age, closes the gap in a split image, turns the corner, skips the formalities and hops to it, *emerging*........on the other side.

and

the cacophony of exact cycles rolls off the forked tongue of chromatic scales and drops its key into the milky way. as the backdrop of staccato sleet falls short of winter, cold slush moves down the muddy inclinations and, like little icy shenanigans, stick to the slow surface of his molecular sled. sliding trombones fracture the silence of mitosis, cracking up the stone face of science. it's as if the motion pulls in both directions at once and tears itself to shreds. the sound of ripping is the movement of stillness. he sulks in the corner of a circle bleeding with immobility.

as the stars shudder with intermittence, the right tracks are covered by a wind of leaves. the routes back to the beginning are hidden by the genetic circumference of identical radii. the machinations of such stationary turbulence vibrate. he shakes with surface tension. his presence is questionable, locked into the key of be. chained by his reaction to inactivity, he's amazed.

and

in this interim, on a crease, vaguely perched on a path that trickles down the folds of sleeping tissue, he is partially aware of the winding scribble that flickers and pulsates in an icicle of harmonics. the density is a shallow thickness that slugs his legs and belts out the musculature of the music and lyrics. he wants to dance but the thin lines crumble and make him look stupid.

and

"I've said it before and I'll say it again and I've said that one thousand times before," he says again and again.

and

just then, which is now, the sameness makes a different impression. this repetition of differences echoes his future remarks. arc angels gently brush the ice caps with their elliptical wings. tangents stick to the skin of the circumference along the sleep meridian. his eyes are heavy, stealing away in the iron darkness. his wife disappears in the lightness. floating to the top ten of regularity, she holds the second hand for balance as she orbits the void. he holds the little hand of slow decline. the marriage of this distance is the back beat of their detachment. they are stuck together by the separateness that adheres to the periphery of love.

and

the next day the focus recedes and gets covered by a dreamy precipitation. a fuzzy rain swallows the ground as birds click their feathers against the soft, silver crystals of evaporation. clouds are the clearest entity present. the rules break in 4/4 and his heart beats in time. each tick makes his blood giggle. each tock knocks his future for a loop. each quick pulse of legato pulls him back to earth with the strength of a root. each mile of his memory remembers the short distance he has gone.

he is under these circumstances. she is moving quickly, skimming the surface of second nature. he is moving imperceptibly, sinking into the sluggishness of minute circumlocution. they touch, briefly, every now and then.

and

now is then.

"would you like to dance?" she asks in a gelatinous voice that pushes her surface to new heights. the thick apex of her crest partially obscures the question but his need to respond to this sensational tug gives him the strength to say 'yes.'

"being positive is a plus," he continues. the words fall from his tongue like little addendums at the end of a deep thought. his phrasing is magnetic and attractive.

and

genetic pools begin to sizzle with a yearning for intersexion. the surface of her configuration pinches in at the middle as his deep concerns fill with light and float to the tip of his body. their lines can now support this commingling. as their hands sweep past the same moment, the overlap gives strength to their gripping fantasy. the dance is imminent.

the criss-crossing of this rhythmic coupling is instantaneous. it's over in a split second. it continues to split in the cellular recollection of otherness that tingles near the edge. a full circle sucks the dance from between their lips. their bodies separate and return to their clockwise positions. the turning of these events is circumstantial.

and

the push and pull of sequence breathes life into a third person. mr. clear is laughing at this vehicle.

"these mechanisms are in opposition to real fiction. the spokes of these cycles are in foreign dialects. how can you expect the uninvited to be cordial?"

he is taken aback. back to his childhood playmates who spoke with his voice. a conscience that is clearly against the science of exactness but is most exact in its exceptions. he and she continue their clockwise repetitions, their rhythmic accumulations and disappearance. the stroke of fantasy is intermittent, a recurrent theme in the score. mr. clear remains the shadow of simultaneity, the one who enters the picture when the door opens and no one is there. the one who pours the hot flesh into abstractions. the one who is the sum of two parts and the difference between right and wrong.

"get to the point. being stuck is one thing. hooking your destiny to the slow certainty of time's smallest hand is another. her quick second glances at substance and her cursory surface are others. but these are snapshots, frozen visions of symbiosis. the fact is, events are small, living tissues. each having a full life of its own. we are only single cells in an organism of eventual outcome. why don't we ever tell the whole story?"

Phil Demise

and

time to reflect. the cyclical nature of Nature is different each time around. the orbit is cylindrical. the seasons return but are never the same. it's the same face of the same clock but the time changes inconstantly.

and

"I'm always in a state of light depression. it's my calma!" he cries.

and

as these words stretch the limits of synapse and twelve tones, the Big Clock strikes oblivion. his grasp slides off the certainty of spacial time, and he falls feet first, legs second, chest third, neck next and head last, into the atmospheric pressure of day to day life. she, upon her next quick passing, not feeling his presence, feels empty, without definition.

"where has our rendezvous gone? where is our periodic dance? why has the pulse stopped? what's going on in our future?" she asks in a thin voice.

and then (which is now), a Spring pops through the winter and severs her hand's relationship to time. she is cut from this cycle and sent hurtling through a fiery coil that spirals down through the earth's contrivance, and lands imbedded, like him, between him, in the imaginary reality of human conditions.

he turns the clock face and pulls the cover over her shivering eyes.

"have we done this before?" she asks.

"not exactly like this," he says, yawning. "we do do this every morning but that was the first time you ever asked that question."

"so what difference does that make?"

"I'm not sure. we'll have to wait and see how the differences add up."

the clock is slow. the alarm sounds off key when it explodes with wakefulness. a new day turns the corner.

and

inside the one
there is the other

inside the other

someone is wearing out
the inside of another

each year reverses

the next memory

forgetting

the ins and outs
of breathing

choking up

bursting like ice
in a pocket of light

stepping backward
into the darkness of almost

that inkling of quickness
that cuts through

the habitual life

now and then
the birth day
of connection
and connotation

from then to now
from now too

from now on

and

sin Sin

half in one tongue
y media en otro

one foot in
(a mouth)
so to speak

one foot without
(a leg)
to stand on

lying down
in formation

we swallow
hard

birds flock close
to the current

wing of flippancy

the flightless curvature
the earth's revolution

the piercing head

a pin, the point
an ache, the angel

an accidental incisor
that punctures the globe

an axis that bites through
the sun's burning thighs

a thin line
balanced
on the edge
of time

the suspension

a light
weightless revelation

the suspense
of the dark

bent on a hidden refraction

the fraction
partially
against the oddity
of a wall
of oracles

the heart beating
itself senseless

a syllable

the tight rope
of a tropical night

the levels of inclination

the elevation
in descent

exposing,
addressing
the naked force

we cannot live
without *(sin)*

and

in the middle of the mundane, somewhere on the edge of the board, a sudden spark of red darkness clips the corners, and rounds out the angles into the soft illusion of an arc angel's vaginal holiness.

entering the white tunnel with a supple erectness, I stand on my head and scale the heights with music, not listening to the echoes that rebound along the cliffs of the future.

the clock, undressed for the occasion, ties a silk thread loosely around its wet hands. it stops, unalarmed, short of the cloudy issue of storms and thunderous clashes.

the present, wrapped in a dream, never finds the time.

the blindfold protects the vision from spilling out.

and

filling the empty space of motion turned 'e,' between the ears, the farce of relativity pushes against the membrane.

thoughts shudder at the thought of an unsound theory; shake at the sight of hearing loss; lose sight of fluidity; bypass the cerebrum; break the record for silence; and crack uncertain smiles.

so sure of its uncertainty, so confident that it will lose confidence, the thrust toward dissolution pounds on a drum of differentials - a positively subtracted coupling of desire and instinct.

lying in a molecule of truth, protected by a dream, we sleep in the wake of restless hunger; in the love of a subatomic middle.

it is an exposure of energy on a grid of description, the graphics of a similar metaphor. it is a regular shadow of unexpected angularity, a mirror with the backdrop depicted on the front. it is the sound of reflection ringing on the tip.

it is the true art of deception.

and

in the folds of the imagination, time surrounds the muscle and addresses the flesh with the indentations of a shadow.

mountains maintain an erect apex of proportion, pulling up on the earth's circles of gravity.

between the cracks, a milky invitation wets the appetite around the silky blindness of syncopation.

the pulse of fantasy beats like a loud clock and wraps its throbbing silence around a black valley that is etched into the memory between the legs of a body of water.

wrapped in the touch of the untouchable, a dream closes its eyes and sleeps.

the idea of a nature made of flesh stands inside my body, building momentum out of hard clouds.

and raining a moist volume onto a flat dimension.

and

a continuum, um um
a stuttering aspect of humankind
each utterance, each syllabic squeak
is part and participle *of*

as, in, to, with

the umbilical sentence
usually for life
and stunning

e pluribus unum

a continuum, um um
untied and united
an orchestrated similarity
a metaphoric difference
chemical voices, molecular strings
atomic percussion, nucleic woodwinds
electric conductors
deoxyribonucleic, etcetera

an unheard of sweet cacophony
an umbrella, a continuum
um um
before and after each occurrence

a singular multiplicity
begins time

and time again

and

in the next scenic moment there is a knock at the door. or rather, a sound of a knock at the door. he looks through the secret eye of an otherwise expressionless portal. there is no one there. exactly no one,

and

Herm Freeman

AFTERWORD

(action)